Family Business in India

A National Asset
THAT NEEDS TO PROFESSIONALIZE

RAJU SWAMY

*"In Business,
We are only as good
as our results"*

INDIA • SINGAPORE • MALAYSIA

Notion Press Media Pvt Ltd

No. 50, Chettiyar Agaram Main Road,
Vanagaram, Chennai, Tamil Nadu – 600 095

First Published by Notion Press 2021
Copyright © Raju Swamy 2021
All Rights Reserved.

ISBN 978-1-63806-789-4

This book has been published with all efforts taken to make the material error-free after the consent of the author. However, the author and the publisher do not assume and hereby disclaim any liability to any party for any loss, damage, or disruption caused by errors or omissions, whether such errors or omissions result from negligence, accident, or any other cause.

While every effort has been made to avoid any mistake or omission, this publication is being sold on the condition and understanding that neither the author nor the publishers or printers would be liable in any manner to any person by reason of any mistake or omission in this publication or for any action taken or omitted to be taken or advice rendered or accepted on the basis of this work. For any defect in printing or binding the publishers will be liable only to replace the defective copy by another copy of this work then available.

Dedicated to my wife, friend, companion, partner,
and critic of 53 years…

Aruna

For her support and encouragement
in allowing me to pursue my professional interests
even during the toughest times

Contents

About the Author *11*
Acknowledgements *13*
Foreword *15*
Foreword *17*

1. My interest in Family Business 21
2. How you may benefit from my book 25
3. Family Business in India 27
4. Frequently occurring issues and solutions 34
5. There is Strength in Unity…in Family Business 41
6. Emotional influences and consequences on decision making in Family Business 44
7. People and Professionalism Promote Profitability in Family Business 46
8. Family Business: Keep employees out of your Conflict Zone 49
9. Family Business: How Professional Employees' Core Specs Change with Business Competitiveness ... 53
10. Daughters and Family Business 55
11. Nepotism 59

12. Succession..61

13. Advice to the Younger Generations of Family Businesses in India: I: If you do not become professional, the Family Business will enter a stagnation phase and find it difficult to survive.......................63

14. Advice to the Younger Generations of Family Business in India on Professionalization: II: Client Experience: *A senior, long-serving non-family manager's letter to the new Younger Generation Directors*...70

15. Advice to the Younger Generations of Family Business in India on Professionalization: III: Client Experience: Your chance to prove that you are Entrepreneurial Leaders, and not just MBs (*Maalik-ke-Bete*/Children of the Owners): Revised Performance/Growth Budgets/Targets/Business Plan of each Division of PluDor for the next three years to start with… 76

16. Advice to the Younger Generations of Family Business in India on Professionalization: IV: Client Experience: The Trivistral Group: Annual Retreat Exercise: "Questions that need answers… from the Fourth Generation…"..................................79

17. Roadmap to Professionalization: The Starting Point: Exercise for Younger Generation Family CEO's Progress Appraisal (Not Started: 0/Outstanding: 10).............83

18. My answers, based on Indian experience, at the Q & A Sessions of the FBAW (Family Business in the Arab World) Conference (Virtual) November 04-05, 2020…(The conference was sponsored by The American University, Sharjah, and by Tharawat Magazine for Family Business) 86

19. The Logic of Business is to Maximize Profit…
    Within a defined and necessary Value-based
    Operating System… 90
20. Entrepreneur CEO Performance Self-Appraisal for
    Business Success..91
21. Warning Signs in a Family Business................................93
22. TIERRRA©..95
23. TIERRRA© Explained – Values and Professionalism
    in Family Business..96
24. Values and Professionalism in Family Business:
    What is the SOP to get Goddess Lakshmi's
    blessings to be successful in business? 98
25. The Family Council 103
26. Client Experience: Melsons Group: Family Council:
    Meeting Checklist..108
27. Client Experience: Functions of the Family Council
    of the Trachmas Group..111
28. Family Constitution – 1 – Introductory 114
29. Family Constitution: 2: Some Directions towards
    evolving a Family Constitution 117
30. Family Constitution: 3: Note to a Client on ground
    rules, specific to questions that came up in
    discussions with them...120
31. Family Constitution: 4: Client Experience:
    Paramdhanam Enterprises: Content Guidelines
    for discussion and integration..123
32. A Note on 'Conflict of Interest' for purposes
    of Shareholders' Agreement/Family Constitution.............127

33. Client Experience (1999): Pioneer Natural
    Products Ltd.: Perpetuating a successful
    Family Business: Strength and Progress Analysis
    and Recommended Action 129

34. Client Experience: National Retail Partners Ltd.:
    A peaceful solution to a uniquely sensitive issue 141

35. Client Experience: Gyanji & Sons: A 92-year-old
    Family Business destroyed by the Third Generation 143

36. Client Experience: AsiaticChem: Avoiding the
    designation trap 146

37. Client Experience: Conflict resolution must also
    result in performance improvement: Progress
    Report to the Statutory Board of Prevexcol
    Exports Ltd. on my ongoing assignment with
    the Promoter Family 148

38. Client Experience: Corporate HR Recommendations
    to Melsons Group: Priority Areas 152

39. Client Experience: The Punjewal Group: A Family
    Business whose deep-rooted negatives drowned
    out the positives and prevented transformation 154

40. Client Experience: PluDor Manufacturing Ltd.:
    First and Second Generation Family Business in
    stagnation, and in serious conflict, but unanimously
    desiring a solution to stay together 164

41. Client Experience: Work in Process: CB Group:
    Charanjibhai Brothers & Co. Ltd (Est. 1905):
    Objective: Peaceful separation, succession…
    so the next and future generations may live
    their lives independently and in harmony 172

42. Client Experience: Mehsangir Engineering: Conflict breeding suspicion: My mail to a client expressing surprise and disappointment over an incident affecting the progress of our joint effort. 181

43. Client Experience: Petran Process Materials Ltd.: Good Families, Good People, Short-sighted by 'Power Shortage', Fight...Winner at great expense, Loser has nothing to show… 184

44. Family Business: Tensions and disharmony rise proportionately with rise in uncertainty and stagnation. 186

45. A Family Office for Family Welfare 189

46. A Model OrgChart for Family Business 192

47. *A Moment of Truth... SWOT Analysis of a 105-year-old Family Business currently managed by the 4th Generation* 194

48. Profit 198

49. So, finally, if you think you need assistance, and if I were to advise and escort you towards desirable change, what would the 'Take-Off' preparation look like? This is exactly the process I have followed with most clients… 200

About the Author

Raju Swamy is an Advisor to Family Business at PROMAG Consultancy Services, which he founded in 1985. Since then, he has consulted across a wide spectrum of Family Businesses, including two that are over 100 years old, across many industries in multiple regions. Prior to founding PROMAG, Raju had nearly 18 years of professional management experience in a reputed family-promoted business group in the Automotive Components Manufacturing Sector. He is an MBA from the first batch of IIMC.

What I have aspired to do...

While it is often quoted that "70 to 80 per cent" of the world's businesses are family-owned, journalists and interviewers of influential media mostly focus on big brand family businesses that are good examples but form just a small percentage of all family businesses in the world. The reasons may be obvious from the media marketing angle, but to me, as an active stakeholder with a mission to 'Upgrade Governance, Competitiveness and Growth' of Family Business across the board, there is more excitement in discovering, assisting and highlighting the "69 to 79 percent" below the tip of the iceberg.

Through my book, for my target audience, and for the younger generation in particular, I attempt to promote a culture of enterprise and achievement, to prevent the safety and security of inherited wealth from suppressing entrepreneurial aspirations and business leadership opportunities.

Acknowledgements

My thanks to my clients over the years who have provided me with the opportunity to pursue my passion for Family Business. Every client enabled me to multiply my knowledge which I could then use in subsequent assignments – and which made it possible for me to write this book with the intention of promoting success in family businesses.

Foreword

*Jayanti Meghjibhai Patel, Executive Chairman,
Meghmani Organics Ltd., Ahmedabad, India*

As one of the Founders, and as the Executive Chairman of the Board at Meghmani Organics, I always envisioned my business running successfully over generations. However, with the emergence of the second generation and the increase in the number of family members directly involved in the family business, we too began to experience issues that required attention. At this point, through a referral, we connected with Raju Swamy to help us overcome the challenges we began to face as a Family Business.

In this contemporary world, wherein enterprising ideas and entrepreneurship flood the minds of individuals, starting a business is the strongest aspiration. Family businesses that have endured and withstood the test of time have truly been a precious asset for our nation's progress. However, it is ironic that more than 70 per cent do not survive past the second generation and only a few make it to the third.

According to Raju Swamy, a capable and committed next generation with a vision that aligns and multiplies the vision of the previous generation is the most important legacy a family business can have. His focus is on achieving continuous profitable growth through 'professionalism' in the management of family-owned businesses. Ultimately, this developmental strategy across generations can increase the longevity of the family business.

Our own transformation over the last five years included eliminating nepotism, defining individual roles with accountability, emphasizing performance with continuous growth, establishing transparency in communication and action among all 'Family Managers' across the hierarchy, through the Family Council, and finally attracting qualified, result-oriented non-family managers into the Family Business.

In his book **"Family Business in India – A National Asset that Needs to Professionalize"** Raju Swamy presents an exhilarating perspective to enable family businesses to ride into the future with ideas that are both logical and are not difficult to implement.

Foreword

By V.K. Surendra, Chairman, VST Group, Bangalore, India

When one looks back at the dynamics and successes of family-run businesses, the role of a consultant and advisor is often overlooked. Many times, when 'right' decisions are made by family business leaders, there are a lot of spirited debates that happen before this 'right' decision is arrived at. Sometimes, a group that has worked together for decades needs an independent and outside perspective to help foster growth within the family business dynamic.

Raju Swamy has played a crucial role in our family business as an independent advisor. He has a successful track record of working with multi-generational family businesses to enable different perspectives to be accepted, without allowing the emotional baggage to cloud decision making.

As the patriarch of a 110-year-old business group, I have the responsibility to groom the next set of leaders to see our business flourish in these changing times. I faced an uphill task to find the right middle ground to please both the emotional and rational side of family expectations on leadership and personal aspirations.

Business leaders face impossible odds of making decisions that are often dynamically opposite in nature. What is assumed to be the right business decision may often turn out to be the wrong family decision, in practice. When you make one choice, you will upset the other. One has an adverse financial impact, whereas the other an adverse emotional impact. How do you weigh one against the other when they are not measurable by the same scale? Think, how much do you value a Rupee gained by upsetting a family member's ego...

With Raju's help and leaning on his three-plus decades of rich, ground-level learnings in this field, our family business was able to find the balance between the older generation and the new. It is his distinctive understanding in not only absorbing unconventional challenges that exist but in also manoeuvring a way through these challenges that matter to a family business leader.

It takes unique skill and comprehension to get leaders to set aside time and to come with an open mind to family discussions. Raju has that skill of understanding with empathy, to create the environment.

Many western scholars have published research on family businesses, but one must acknowledge in traditional countries like India, where true capitalism is in its infancy, western research has limited acceptability.

Universally, you will agree that maturity and age have only a little direct correlation to business acumen and decision making. Yet, unlike in the corporate world, in the family business, this perception often plays a larger-than-life role. Decisions that will never be taken in a western capitalistic boardroom setting, are often expected to be taken in an Indian family business environment for the sake of family harmony.

This is the challenge I faced in finding the right balance between keeping multi-generational family members content and motivated, while also making them see the larger picture and moving our businesses forward. With Raju's help and valuable learnings, I was able to navigate the balance between the boardroom and the living room, while staying true to family values and dynamics in this unique business setting.

The Core Issue of a Family Business

(As described by the patriarch of an old, large, traditional, and reputed branded fast moving product manufacturer in India)

"We are 16 active family members in the Family Business. We all fetch and store water in a traditional water pot, and drink from it when we are thirsty. The problem is we do not know who fills how much and who drinks how much. And we are afraid to ask."

(Translated from Hindi)

1

My interest in Family Business

Prior to starting my consulting business, 35 years ago, I was fortunate that my primary management experience covering nearly 18 years, soon after I graduated from Business School (IIMC) in 1966, was with the ANAND Group, an extremely progressive, professionally managed Family-promoted Business Group. The ANAND Group is a leader in the Automotive Components Industry in India, now possibly in the world. And the real bonus was that I got to work directly with the very enlightened Chairman of the Group, Deep C. Anand, for many years. Deep Anand's autobiography 'Upstream' is a must-read for upcoming leaders of family businesses.

My experience in the ANAND Group encompassed a wide spectrum of responsibilities related to building the future of the Business Group, including new projects, and the development of people, and markets, and the importance of growth. Experience in marketing ranged from selling in a region to being the Country Head. This varied, hands-on management experience has had a great influence on my consulting style.

Soon after, when I set up my consulting practice, my first Family Business Client was N. Ranga Rao & Sons, the manufacturers of Cycle Brand Agarbathis (Incense sticks). The senior partners, R. Guru, and R.N. Murthy introduced me to the importance of a deeper understanding of the behind-the-scenes family relationships, values, and vibes that inevitably influence the dynamics of the family business. Once again, this Family Business Group, known popularly as NR

& Sons, is today, successfully firing on all cylinders, and continues to be India's largest, and one of the world's leading production and marketing houses in the area of fragrances and fragrance-based products. Cycle Brand is the No. 1 brand in the incense stick industry. 'Succession planning' was a notable achievement of this Family Business Group with the professional and smooth handing over of management to the third generation in the early part of this century.

Experience across the world shows that family businesses generally progress to the second generation, but, only an optimistic 30 per cent or less manage to survive beyond them to the third generation.

The obvious reason is that education, exposure, living standards, aspirations multiply in succeeding generations. If a family business has not kept pace with products, market, and industry relevance, and when the growth does not match the aspirations of a more demanding generation, succession becomes a hurdle resulting in the family business struggling to survive.

Additional issues affecting the succession and longevity of family business include the decline in the percentage of the younger generation available in the population profile in most of the traditional industrial nations of Europe. In the USA, succession issues in many family businesses arise from the complexities of accommodating children born of multiple marriages. This could be true of some cases in Europe too.

Each time I have consulted with a new family business, my appreciation and understanding of the dynamics of family and business, and business and family multiplied significantly. Guru and Murthy's early lessons were reinforced by my discovering repeatedly how relationships and other issues within the family have a significant influence on the management and decision-making process within the family business.

Fortunately, most of my clients have been serious about wanting change and provided me with the right opportunity to practice my beliefs and help implement them. All my work has been multi-generational.

Between the years 2000 and 2014, I also had opportunities to interact and compare notes with Prof. John Ward during his brief annual visits to India as the primary faculty for the Annual CII FBN Family Business Conventions. Prof. Ward is considered a leading authority on Family Business Governance. His case study on the Murugappa Group is a 'pioneering classic' in Indian Family Business studies.

The content of my book includes the reproduction of selected recommendations that I have made to my clients – identity hidden, of course – that formed part of the process of advising them, in each situation. My primary target audience includes key members/heads of business families who may, through my writings, recognize their symptoms and derive solutions to move forward. However, my experience has taught me that each family is one of a kind... stereotypes are rare.

I do believe in, and promote, certain 'Core Values of Family Business' branded by me as TIERRRA, the Crown Jewel of Family Business Governance. TIERRRA embeds Trust, Integrity, Ethics, Relationships, Reputation, Results, Accountability. Implementing TIERRRA helps develop professionalism in leadership and management.

A phenomenon that I have observed: Even while it is often quoted that "70 to 80 percent" of the world's businesses are family-owned, journalists and interviewers mostly focus on big brand family businesses that form just a small percentage of all family businesses in the world. The reasons may be obvious from the publishers' marketing angle, but to me, as an active stakeholder with a mission to 'Upgrade Governance, Competitiveness and Growth' of family businesses, there is more excitement in discovering and assisting the "69 to 79 percent" below the tip of the iceberg.

To me, a Family Business is more interesting than a business of any other kind. A Family Business continues to be more 'human', more 'real', and has the potential to 'multiply' from within. I enjoy the challenge of finding new ways of keeping 'The Family Business Growth Highways' free of potholes and unregulated crossings, to enable emerging generations to stay on track and reach newer destinations.

2

How you may benefit from my book...

This is not a 'textbook', nor is it a scholarly work based on interviews and desk research. This is a book that narrates my actual experience with Family Business clients in varied businesses, across industries that were established from anywhere between 30 to 120 years ago. I am a hands-on 'Consultant Implementor', who identifies the problems that clients have, suggests solutions, and works with them closely to help with the implementation.

Most of my clients are well educated, run good businesses with good potential, and are serious about improving the way they manage their businesses. As multi-generational, multiple families, they have a basic desire to stay together and therefore seek my assistance. Since they are all experienced businessmen in a competitive world, and their time is precious, they are also clear that I must deliver value. And, to me, delivering value is about creating a positive family business governance structure that also simultaneously improves business performance and results.

I have also had a couple of clients with a negative streak who seem bent on self-destruction because of their extreme interpersonal and inter-family disputes arising from lack of trust, and disputes over money and wealth. One of them was resolved and, for the other, there is has no hope of resolution. Both case studies are included in this book.

These presentations are my views based on consolidated experiences as well as specific client experiences. I expect that many answers you are looking for will become evident in my writings.

I do not disclose the actual names of my clients to maintain their privacy and because of the sensitive nature of the subject. However, all descriptions, interpretations, and advice represent an accurate reflection of my work with clients. *I often use an expression 'FMB' which is short for 'Family Member in Business' and this includes anyone from the families involved in the Family Business who is specifically participating in the management of the Family Business.*

3

Family Business in India

There was a time, during my growing-up years, in the 1950s and '60s when what mattered in India was the 'government', and everything in India was great because of the 'government'. A 'sarkari' job was much sought after for money, security, pension, holidays, and the absence of pressure to deliver performance of any kind. Simultaneously, the message was also clear that 'business' and 'businessmen' lived only to exploit the poor ignorant workers by trying to make 'profit' on everything they sold. 'Profit' was a bad word and 'business' was always suspect.

What many may not be aware of is that the government – with good intentions – set up 'temples of modern India' in the form of huge public sector enterprises that provided employment and wages to millions of our countrymen. Government employing and paying wages was considered good, but employees desiring to spend their money on consumables to better their living standards was considered bad. Any person wanting to set up a business to cater to the consumption demands of these new earning employees had to take permission from the government, and production had to be restricted as per norms set by the government. These norms were based on the 'socialist' view that consumption should be driven by moral standards, and businessmen should be prevented from enjoying the unfair and exploitive fruits of enterprise. All interpretations were by the government, not by the logic of demand and supply and competition and natural market pricing – but a vague belief in an unproven 'socialistic pattern of society'.

The politicians and bureaucrats of an independent India, almost up until 1990, failed to understand that privately owned businesses, over 75 per cent of which were family-owned, were actually national assets providing employment and wealth-building opportunities for a developing India. They could not see beyond the short-sightedness of their political masters.

The result was the development of an 'Inflationary, Shortage Economy' from the creation of millions of direct and indirect wage-earning employees in the government, in public sector enterprises, while restricting the availability of consumables through a 'License Raj' – a permit system thriving on bribery and corruption. Thus emerged India's 'Black Market Economy'. Simultaneously, extremely high corporate taxes and income taxes levied on income and profits beyond the governments' narrow definition gave birth to large scale tax evasion that only added even more support to the 'Black Market Economy'.

The Indian economy became a strange mix of more and more people finding employment in the government and public sector companies who had money to spend, and traditional and new entrepreneurs conducting business profitably through a black-market economy (created by the politics of misapplied socialism mixed with lack of economic common-sense). It was not uncommon during those times for milk-food for babies to be in short supply and for scooters to command a premium of 50% or more in 'black' and a waiting period of ten years!

Some good developments were also there, like in the higher education sector. Unfortunately, here again, full circle follow-through solutions were missing. For example, it appeared as though the IITs were set up to feed the American industry as employment opportunities in India did not match up to the superior quality of engineering graduates that the IITs began turning out.

It is during this type of constricted economic environment that the mass launching of what are called 'family businesses' today, happened. Before this period there were a few pioneering family business houses belonging to the 'branded' rich, successful, and politically influential families: Tata, Birla, R.P. Goenka, Godrej, Shriram, Singhania, Walchand, Kirloskar, Mafatlal, Mahindra, and a few others.

From the mid-1950s to July 1991, we can see that Indian Business functioned in a 'protected economy' with little or no competition, highly restricted new investment, and subject to total government control. Smaller businesses in manufacturing and in trading were at the mercy of Factory Inspectors, Excise Duty Inspectors, and Inspectors under the Shops & Establishment Act. And everyone in business also had to 'take care' of the Income Tax and Sales Tax people. Obviously, recovery of costs arising from pleasing government functionaries was possible only through tax evasion. Overall, within this system that enabled a stagnant but profitable business culture, a family business was able to survive.

Most business families nurtured their businesses in a relatively comfortable, unadventurous, non-competing, elders-know-best, and 'salaam maalik' organizational environment.

Then 'July 1991' happened! India had to pledge tonnes of gold to avoid defaulting on sovereign debt. There was also a foreign exchange shortage crisis affecting strategic imports. The impact of years of negative economic policy hit the government so hard that change was inevitable: With immediate effect, investment, domestic or foreign, was welcome, competition was welcome, imports were welcome. The economy was to be market-driven, and the services sector was to be encouraged. One can say real independence came to India in July 1991 when Indian enterprise was let loose to function in freedom.

A whole new breed of entrepreneurs entered the business scene in the form of enterprising qualified professionals with domain expertise and a global reach. Multinationals with global brands entered a starved consumer market and set up manufacturing in India. Indian consumers for the first time had access to even fruits from all over the world. There were both opportunities, and challenges.

The greatest impact of 1991 was on family businesses. They had to confront competition and had to adapt to a new business and management culture to survive. Even traditional old and large family business houses faced disruption. If one were to compare the Top 40 between 1951 and 1990, at least 16 well-known family businesses disappeared or were far lower on the list by 2016.

At the same time, a new breed of younger generation entrepreneurs and family businesses entered the scene led by 21st-century visionaries with competence in emerging new areas of Technology, Telecom, Energy, Transportation, and Services. They had faith in Professional Management, the world was their market, and their goal was to excel continuously in the performance and growth of their enterprises.

If one examines the ET 500 2019 Ranking, something interesting is seen: nearly 40 per cent of companies in the Top 100 are family businesses while in the bottom 100, it is nearly 90 per cent! There are two conclusions that can be drawn from this data: in the ET TOP 100, non-family businesses are ahead on size and performance variables, while, as we go lower down towards 500, the percentage of family businesses over all other businesses is overwhelmingly high. To get promoted to the Top 100 and Top 200, family businesses will obviously have to improve both on management and on performance. Of course, the Top 100 and Top 200 also include a fair number of public sector enterprises, banks, and finance-related companies.

In both the Sensex S&P 100 and in Nifty 50, family businesses constitute over 50 per cent of the listed companies included.

Family Business, small, medium, and large, will always be there within the foreseeable future, as a great source of strength for the Indian economy, creating employment and wealth, and generating significant revenue for the government through the tax route. Family businesses are essential for the economic well-being of India.

However, with few exceptions, all family businesses that are more than 50 years old need to change the way they do business and update their organizational and work culture. These businesses were nurtured pre-1991 in a competition-free 'protection' era with a succession pipeline based on nepotism and complacency rather than on merit or competence. Progress has been more towards maintaining the status quo than on growth.

Based on the many family businesses I have been exposed to, there are five conditions I have noticed often:

- First, a family business involving multiple families and multiple generations faces complex survival issues when growth is not adequate to accommodate all the family members who think it is their right to be an important part of the family business, irrespective of qualifications and competence.

- Second, I would strongly advise any elder generation founder or patriarch that when he is ready to permanently move 'upstairs' – if he has two sons, leave behind two businesses, and if there are three sons, leave behind three businesses. Peace among equals is easier with a 'Patriarch' overseeing the family business. Without a 'Patriarch' to play a balancing role, I am not exaggerating when I say 'governance' can be reduced to Jungle Raj.

- Third, when differences arise from the distribution of money, wealth, power, and nepotism, and not from business performance and accountability or visions for the future, there is no hope for the survival of the family business.

- Fourth, even when there are serious differences of opinion about the management of the family business, or about the sharing of 'power', as long as there is financial integrity within the multiple families, it is easier to find solutions. Even separations can be peacefully negotiated and implemented. Two of my larger clients taught me this lesson.

- Lastly, some years ago, the Chairman of an old and reputed Family Business in a traditional, fast-moving product, defined his primary issue in these words: "*We are 16 active family members in the family business. We all fetch and store water in a traditional water pot, and drink from it when we are thirsty. The problem is we do not know who fills how much and who drinks how much. And we are afraid to ask.*" He said it in colloquial Hindi and left me wonderstruck at how easily he had in one sentence defined accurately what can take a hundred pages in a scholarly book!

My approach to the transformation of family businesses from the traditional passive and comfortable to the modern is based on the premise that critical problems of a family in business are best resolved by focusing on business performance and growth. It is finally the 'business' that will provide the resources for building family security and wealth, and for wellbeing and peace.

"Growth is the Key; Stagnation Kills." It is mostly stagnation that snowballs into conflict, and accumulates dirt, and leaves behind the unpleasant precipitate that could break up a family business, and the family behind the business.

4

Frequently occurring issues and solutions

From the 1990s, family business issues have become particularly important given the need to compete, survive, and grow in a liberal 'survival of the fittest' business climate coupled with an increasingly demanding internal family environment.

Traditionally, in a less high-pressure business environment, most small and medium family-owned and owner-managed businesses have been living with their problems either on grounds of protecting 'family prestige' or simply because of a feeling of helplessness in a closed hierarchical society.

However, trends can be noticed in the case of most of the relatively 'medium-to-larger' closely held, family-managed businesses with recognizable brand equity that have emerged over the last 50 years and more. Most of my clients fall in this category... at least two of them are over 100 years old. All of them have been 'founder-managed' or single-family managed, to start with.

With the traditional hierarchy of the single-family in place (father and unmarried sons/elder brother and younger brothers) and with good business performance and cash flow, and mutual understanding, peace has prevailed. In most such enterprises, and particularly where manufacturing and international business and trading are involved, the 'family managers' are well educated and business-competitive. Work and responsibility are shared informally with mutual understanding.

Over time, however, with the business track record being good, and with relative peace and mutual understanding within the family, complacency on the family front sets in.

Mutual understanding is taken for granted, and problems if any between the family members in the business are swept under the carpet or postponed for future consideration because business pressures on a day-to-day basis leave no time for attending to such issues.

So long as the business grows, and wealth accumulation is possible, and cash flows are good, it is 'business is as usual'. But, below the surface, individual feelings do get bottled up. Even then, if the enterprise continues to be with members of a single family, not much damage may be caused at least for a few years.

The real issues begin to emerge with the growth and extension of the family with marriages, children, and the concurrent increase in responsibility and commitment of each son or brother to their respective families. Internal pressures now come bubbling to the surface.

Pressures become more serious when the patriarch of the family passes on. Once all the sons or brothers are married and have their own families, the enterprise is no longer 'single-family owned' – it is now owned by more than one family with multiple vested interests in the business.

When the third generation is ready to enter the business, and the business has not grown adequately to service the increase in numbers of potentially business-active members of the 'families', bottled up issues can become explosive. And the business can almost reach breaking point unless damage control exercises are carried out and an acceptable solution emerges.

Part of the problem is that family-owned and managed enterprises have been inducting into the business – as a matter of 'duty' – new cost-incurring but profit-sharing family members at a rate higher than their business growth rate.

Each induction must necessarily result in value addition to the business. However, more new family members with higher standards of living but without concurrent value addition capability, dependent on a stagnant or slow-growth business, means greater chances of poor performance, conflict and stress.

There are many other issues confronting family enterprises today, including induction of wives, daughters, daughters-in-law into the business, 'leadership among equals', and 'professionalization' both in terms of attitude, knowledge, and result-orientation of family managers and in terms of inducting qualified 'external to family' professionals who will require to be handled with care.

In many family enterprises, there is a reluctance to induct proven, intelligent professionals.

Many family enterprises, particularly the older ones, have continued to run their businesses internally with a feudal undercurrent that encourages subservience and consequent mediocrity in employee quality and performance standards.

Unfortunately, functioning in such an environment every day over the years can lead family managers to attribute to themselves an exaggerated estimate of their knowledge and performance capacities. This tends to be tested often in the tough market and the external world much to the disadvantage of the family enterprise.

The other particularly important issue is 'succession', which is a very significant part of the 'planning for change' process.

If 'wealth' is not a serious issue, and this is so in some of the older family enterprises, it is the desire for 'power' that vitiates the family business environment and complicates any effort at achieving 'fair succession'. The struggle for power, and concurrent nepotism, with the absence of accountability, together form a lethal mix that prevents merit-based succession.

The 'power struggle' becomes even more vicious in a stagnant business situation when there is less to share, both in money and in management space. Individual partner-families' desire to independently make up for losses through parallel business opportunities promote situations of 'conflict of interest' and disturb inter-family relationships.

Retirement, or 'Letting go', has become a somewhat serious and ironic problem particularly in recent years as older generations are fitter in their late sixties, and in their seventies, even while younger generations aspire for greater responsibilities in their thirties and forties.

In many cases, 'Letting go' to ease 'succession' can be facilitated by an attractive and productive Retirement Policy where the 'elder' will continue to enjoy certain perks of higher management, including financial support for continuing to maintain one's social and economic status within business and community circles.

It is somewhat inevitable that being confronted with difficulties in achieving 'growth with harmony', in an extremely competitive business environment, family-owned-and-managed enterprises, will have to rapidly multiply the process of change in the following directions:

1. Family Enterprises need to plan for their future. Sounds obvious but is missing even among 'modern and educated' members of family enterprises. I have more than once been surprised how easily even 'MBAs' in the younger generation begin to enjoy the comfort of 'walking in' to a position of power (and perks) without accountability to deliver, as they begin to enjoy 'nepotistic' protection!

2. Family enterprises need to 'formalize' their management structure of business-active family members/partners/directors of the enterprise in terms of role definition, functional responsibility, authority, reporting, accountability and performance appraisal, and the reward system. Again, obvious but over-looked.

3. Family enterprises need to match the enterprise/business purpose, objectives and plans with the requirements both of the incoming younger generation and of the existing partners to be able to cope with the increasing complexities of running the family business and business in general.

4. Family enterprises need to evolve a 'Management Procedure and Code of Conduct' package, with external assistance if necessary, that could evolve into a 'Partnership Pact' or a 'Governance Code' or a 'Family Constitution' or a 'Family Protocol' to sustain unity during and after the change process on a long-term basis:

    - as the family business grows, across many locations,

    - as the number of family members in the business increases to a level where traditional and frequent face-to-face interpersonal contact is no longer possible.

5. 'Succession' as a process must not be translated into over-simplified nepotism or a whimsical exercise in which a dominant family member forces a decision deliberately overlooking merit, and others go along to maintain the peace. A good 'succession plan' will restructure the enterprise to harness the leadership skills and potential of competent members of the family, and therefore help create new growth opportunities.

6. Tax planning as part of a restructuring strategy, consequent to succession planning, is necessary and important. However,

tax planning must not override the need to sustain family business unity for future generations. To re-emphasize, focusing on sustaining family business unity is more important than saving tax as the primary motivation in restructuring for 'unity with growth'.

7. When there are unaccounted illegal business transactions within a family business, distrust multiplies. While questionable business practices might have existed traditionally from the past, the concurrent need for secrecy through highly controlled and restricted information flow to the bare minimum is obviously not possible as families multiply. Elimination of illegal business practices coupled with transparency in communication is good for sustaining the Family Business through mutual trust, and in building a long-term legacy for succeeding generations.

8. In most cases, feelings of financial and social insecurity among either less advantaged or less competent family members, and ageing family members, in the enterprise, can result in ego clashes, lack of trust, destructive nepotism, and other obstacles to the survival of the family business. To a large extent, this can be pre-empted by establishing family-constituted and professional advice assisted entities driven by a Family Constitution to ensure a process of cooperative wealth management, of ensuring minimum economic support, of protection from unforeseen disasters and calamities, and of providing personal and social security in old age.

   8.1. The 'Family Office' can be the facilitator and administrator of this process of ensuring family well-being, and of peace within the family.

   8.2. Such a process, if carefully planned and constituted, can promote meritocracy as the key driver as far as the business part of the family is concerned since less competent family members are taken care of otherwise, through the Family Office.

9. **Conclusion:**

   9.1. **It is finally the 'business' that will provide the resources for building family security and wealth, as well as well-being and peace. Therefore, business must be governed, strategized, and structured to grow profitably in perpetuity.**

   9.2. **Growth is the greatest driver, Stagnation the greatest enemy.**

   9.3. **Growth supports and perpetuates Unity, always.**

Family businesses by their very nature are entrepreneurial. They are necessary constituents of a dynamic society riding on a rising economic wave. I will not be exaggerating when I say that India – minus passing hiccups – continues to be in the process of emerging into a spanking new entrepreneurial society where, paradoxically, it will be even more difficult to survive, if you have *not* done your homework, but if you do your homework, then it could be NIRVANA all the way!

Many family enterprises across the country have already initiated the change process. There are also many examples today to prove that in an unsuppressed creative business environment, a flood of successful first-generation entrepreneurs are emerging with a multiplier effect.

The horizon of opportunity has widened like never before, truly into a "borderless world". Family enterprises need to recognize this fact and initiate the change process. They have little choice, for markets do not wait. It is *always* a race against time.

5

There is Strength in Unity...in Family Business

From my experience and understanding of Family Business, success in resolving issues depends totally on a strong and spontaneous desire to stay together. Often this desire is challenged by business setbacks and consequent attempts at fixing blame. And unfortunately, even as times change for the better, residue from the blame-game can clog the pipeline. Therefore, a really strong and spontaneous desire to stay together must be supported by self-sealing chemistry that seals the surface cracks as they emerge before the structure begins to break.

It is important, therefore, to understand family and family business sensitivities to preserve or strengthen Unity:

1. Family and family business must be mutually exclusive. Personal attachments and opinions based on family considerations cannot override professional decision-making. In a competitive business environment, the family will be the loser if decisions are devoid of merit or compromises are made to buy peace at any cost.

2. Sometimes, having grown up together and knowing each other too well, people in the family could be taken for granted. Members of a family in business need professional appreciation, new opportunities, professional up-gradation, performance rewards, and other ways of motivation to perform beyond the ordinary.

3. History should not stifle the future. 'Ghosts from the past' are the biggest enemies of family business. And their influence multiplies with time even as they co-exist with the blurred vision of a family seeking small, short-term victories. 'Ghosts' from history must be identified and buried so deep that they disappear for all time without recall, leaving a positive legacy for the future generation. A less-stressed, healthy, secure, and peaceful family is better-enabled to take fair professional decisions in business for the benefit of all.

4. A family freed from 'ghosts of the past' presents a united front to the professional managers and employees in the family business. They will not be diverted from their focus on work, innovation, and push for growth. 'Organizational politics' raises its head in an environment of uncertainty and stagnation caused by confused and conflicting leadership.

5. *In the ultimate analysis, 'conflict' is a sickness that threatens life and livelihood. Even more so in a closed family situation.*

Even more so when we are in our fifties, and sixties, and beyond. Energy is better spent on promoting a successful future for all.

This is certainly not new knowledge. This is a call for translating knowledge into action. Before time runs out on you.

6

Emotional influences and consequences on decision making in Family Business

1. Positive emotional behaviour and expression are present as a natural consequence of sustained growth and success in any ownership model, primarily because when success exceeds failure it is affordable, and adds to the feel-good ambience within the organization. However, a prolonged recession or an unexpected business downturn can change everything overnight.

2. In a family business, particularly if facing stagnation and personal financial pressures, coupled with questions of establishing 'ownership' for poor business performance, emotions become strategic…the quality of emotions ranging from defensive to aggressive to blackmail.

3. Something that has surprised me no end is the emotional blackmail strategy used by otherwise pioneering 'founders' of the family business when it comes to letting go, either because of old age or because of performance issues. When the third generation is ready to come in and they see the second generation looking helpless, seeds of conflict and break-up are many times planted by the erstwhile founders themselves because of their insecurities about letting go.

4. A founder of a large family business once confessed to me that his eldest son was fit and ready to take over except that the founder himself was scared of what he would be reduced

to once he handed over power to his son. Strangely, in many family businesses even today, fear of emotional eruption prevents discussion and formulation of a 'retirement policy', and consequently, even 'succession planning' becomes an emotional issue to be avoided to prevent unpleasantness.

5. Nepotism in the family business is also driven by emotional considerations. Merit, and consequent business growth prospects, get sacrificed.

6. *Wherever emotions dominate ownership and management decision making, knowledge, values, logic, common sense, professionalism, speed, business motivation, and competitiveness are sacrificed to kill growth and, instead, promote business stagnation, conflict, and instability.*

7

People and Professionalism Promote Profitability in Family Business

1. **People:**

    1.1. In highly family-controlled public companies where critical top management positions are held by Family Members in Business (FMB), it is difficult to attract and retain the best or the most appropriate level of professional managers.

    1.2. Professional managers who do work for such family-controlled businesses might find it difficult to express an honest opinion or to be fair in their interactions up and down the line or even to deliver the best they are capable of, in the face of unaccountable, authoritarian, untested, or unverified decision-making from FMBs heading the division or organization.

    1.3. Professional managers can become even more confused when the ultimate responsibility or accountability for the performance of a division or organization is left compromised and undefined to cater to family sensitivities. Organizational and family politics will most certainly compromise performance under these circumstances.

2. 'Professionalism', in the Family Council, and in FMBs:

2.1. When FMBs – Family Members in Business – occupy positions of power and authority because of family pressures and sensitivities, and less on a proven track record of merit, 'professionalism' in terms of accountability for quality and delivery of performance most certainly gets diluted.

2.2. When family pressures and sensitivities prevent appropriate and timely corrective action to be taken against questionable discipline, inadequate performance, and poor leadership, professionalism is as good as dead.

2.3. When family dynamics prevent result-backed high-performing FMBs from being recognized and rewarded, not only will professionalism be thwarted, new and more powerful seeds of discord will get planted within the family business.

2.4. Conflict of Interest also most certainly compromises professionalism.

3. Profitability:

3.1. The difficulty in attracting and retaining good external non-family professionals with the required domain expertise and capacity, adversely affects operations and the quality and delivery of desired results, and therefore affects profitability.

3.2. The absence of professionalism in FMBs prevents the maximization of profitability through suppression of merit-supported, fact-supported decision-making.

3.3. Decisions based on family pressures and sensitivities against organizational needs, kill or dilute profitability.

3.4. Conflict of Interest dilutes profitability.

The above points summarize the need for a family business, particularly a listed company, with external stakeholders, to arrive at a productive fusion of family business strengths with professional discipline, to maximize profitability, today, and well into the future.

8

Family Business: Keep employees out of your Conflict Zone

In a Family Business, it takes little to ignite a fire...particularly when business is not too good, and the family environment is undergoing tension resulting from uncertainty... In bad times, the Family Business is like a 'matchbox', and often the employees become 'matchsticks'!

Most employees are good human beings primarily pursuing their livelihood and, in the process, trying to meet their aspirations and responsibilities. Like in any cross-section of society there are also those who are happiest keeping others unhappy. In a Family Business, conflict and misunderstanding are fodder for such employees to thrive. What can be the causes:

1. Lack of unity in leadership.

2. Developing a 'my man' 'your man' identity for various employees.

3. Discussing family business issues in front of employees, passing remarks, openly blaming other family colleagues, implying wrong practices, and generally spreading uneasiness and insecurity within the organization multiplies the internal problems of the family business.

4. In such a situation, certain types of employees become conduits for carrying tales, spreading rumours, exploiting a family member's frustration or anger through flattery,

and generally making themselves 'important', and secure. Unfortunately, such types of employees are normally those who are professionally incompetent, and therefore the need to cover up through these negative acts.

5. Many times, disgruntled employees who feel they have been unfairly treated may also add fuel to the fire.

6. There are also employees who are exposed to a family business's possible unethical dealings, who will exploit the situation.

7. There are even some employees who are so used to surviving and doing well in a family conflict situation that they actually feel insecure about any imminent positive change. There was this great Hollywood film a few years ago, 'One Flew Over the Cuckoo's Nest': It features a mental hospital administered by a domineering Matron for many years. She has been part of this mental hospital for so long that any change makes her insecure. One day, there is a new patient who has the will to fight his way out of his condition and begins to show signs of improvement. To the Matron, this is a threat to her position and security. What will happen if her mad inmates become normal? She will lose her power… for she enjoys power only so long as her inmates are 'mad'. She gets obsessed with this threat to her status quo and does everything in her power to sabotage the new inmate's efforts… and succeeds. As I stated earlier, *there could be similar loyal, long-serving, hard-working, up-from-the-ranks but insecure employees who may find security in a conflict or 'status-quo' situation in a Family Business.*

8. It is important for family members in the business to be level-headed and stick together when significant changes are taking place for results to be positive.

9. It is often true that every time partners or directors of a Family Business get together, whatever the occasion, it can become a Board Meeting. So, imagine, if the Chairman of the Family Business, his son and nephew are travelling by car from Malabar Hill to Vikhroli, or to Mulund, or to Thane, a trip of not less than one hour, whether in an 'Ambassador' or Dodge Kingsway in the old days, in a Jaguar or Mercedes or Maybach today, what will they be discussing? And who else is listening? The 'driver' (or chauffeur in certain countries), of course. And this will happen even if they are driving from South Extension to Faridabad, from Rajaji Nagar to Electronic City, or Nungambakam to Velachery, or from Jubilee Hills to Cyberabad…

In the 1960s and '70s, in Mumbai, there was an immensely powerful – and feared – Union Leader whose forte was to threaten violent strikes – and even closure of the factory – if his demands were not met. His knowledge of what managements of companies, family businesses and others were planning or discussing was such that most times he was always a step ahead. His core 'Intelligence Network' consisted of company-employed personal drivers working for Company Chairmen, MDs, Directors, General Managers, and drivers for group pick-ups and drops. Drivers knew everything!

The 'driver' example is given here only because it is easy to explain and to understand. Today, there are many, many avenues of information leakage with lot more 'intelligence' in proximity … human, wired, invisible and unknown.

The ultimate solution is to have nothing to hide, with professional performance that stands out and makes people proud to be working for the company. Satisfied employees working in healthy, performing, rewarding business environments will do everything to protect their Management.

In summary, family members involved in the management of the business must ensure togetherness, avoid unguarded and loose statements, spend enough time together to be on the same wavelength, and be focused on success and well-being of the family business, and of the people depending on you, both within the family and within the organization – for it takes very little to ignite a fire in a family business.

9

Family Business: How Professional Employees' Core Specs Change with Business Competitiveness…

1. Traditional: "Landlord"/"Zamindar"

    1.1. Authority ("Ownership")

    1.2. *Loyalty + Subservience + Accountability without authority*

2. Traditional: Business: Monopoly/No Competition

    2.1. Seniority + *Loyalty* + Authority

    2.2. *'Subservience' minimized with emphasis on 'Loyalty'*

3. Traditional: Monopoly/Some Competition

    3.1. Seniority + Loyalty + *Competence* + Authority

    3.2. *'Competence' becomes a necessary add-on….*

4. Emerging: Monopolistic/Significant Competition/Pricing + Profit Pressures

    4.1. Seniority + Loyalty + Competence + *Accountability* + Authority

    4.2. *Accountability becomes indispensable…..even while supporting 'Seniority' and 'Loyalty'….*

5. **Emerging: Free Market/Intense Competition/Cost + Pricing + Profit Pressures/Growth/Viability/Scaling Economics/HR Challenges**

   5.1. *Commitment* + Competence + Accountability + Authority

   5.2. **Competence + Accountability + Authority (Desperate 'no choice' situation)**

   5.3. *Commitment replaces 'Seniority + Loyalty'.......in current practices towards 'Professionalization'......*

10

Daughters and Family Business

Yes, there are still many family businesses where daughters do not get to play a key role. However, it is also true that in most enlightened families today, keeping daughters out of the family business is not really about gender discrimination. Often, if daughters are kept out of the primary family business, there are alternative profitable or supportive businesses or assets created for daughters, so that they get their fair share of benefits or more.

There can be sensitive family relationship issues that determine induction or otherwise of an educated, competent daughter into the main family business:

1. At the early stage of a family business, if the 'family' is the founder, his unmarried sons, and unmarried daughters, there is no problem. The entire dynamics of the family business revolves around one family.

2. When the daughter gets married, the son-in-law – an additional family member, with an external connection, joins the family. There is a new 'self-interest' that may not coincide with the original family business interests. In such a situation, at least two good clients of mine took the following steps:

    2.1. Assisted the daughter to start an independent business through asset transfers and funding.

    2.2. They made sure that their daughter's assets are exclusively under her control.

    2.3. External (Non-Family) Advisory Assistance was enabled if specifically requested by the daughter.

    2.4. The assets and funding arrangements were also designed carefully to ensure that should there be a problem in the marriage, including divorce, the daughter could take care of herself.

3. In business families where the founder is enlightened and progressive, and where there are only daughters, there are good examples where the family business is managed by the daughters, again educated and competent, and where the sons-in-law have no role.

4. There are also examples of old and prominent family businesses where female members, whatever the relationship, have been kept out of the family business. The female members have financial entitlements including shares in the family business but do not have any board or management roles. The reason is again the possible mismatch with the self-interest of the

son-in-law that could affect the well-being and unity of the established family business.

5. In some family businesses, married daughters are provided specific non-decision-making positions away from the mainstream organization structure, by way of creating an income stream.

6. The dynamics of family relationships change even when the founder's sons get married. The daughters-in-law also bring in new equations that change the way the original family of the founder functioned. Every time a son gets married, a potential new family is created with its own self-interest. From a 'single-family' family business, there is now a 'multi-family' family business.

7. The dynamics of family relationships change, both when the daughter/daughters get married, and when the son/sons get married.

8. In the traditional joint family system there were clear but unwritten power-sharing, task allocation, and interaction rules of a feudal leadership structure that suited less mobile, non-industrial, agriculture-based small-town economies. This joint family system breaks down in aspirational industrial societies of a larger economic system where educated married daughters prefer independence from the repressive joint family structure.

In summary, because of sensitive family dynamics that can cause harm to an existing family business, married daughters may be kept out. However, daughters cannot be deprived of all entitlements and of alternate business opportunities by the business family they are born into.

In the case of unmarried daughters, based on their education and competence, active opportunities in the family business are provided. However, their future role will depend on their marriage plans. At least one of my larger clients has two unmarried daughters, professionally qualified, and fully involved in the management of the family business. There are no sons in the family. The father would not like to see either of the daughters exit from the management of the family business. He is proud of them. It will be interesting to see what happens!

In the not-too-distant future, with family businesses turning professional in terms of mixing merit and performance, zero gap in education and competence levels between sons and daughters, communication modes changing, and locational flexibility, I can see this gender discrimination having no further value.

11

Nepotism

In the context of Indian family culture, parents wanting to help their children get a good start in life and in their careers is obviously something good and is still widely prevalent. And likely to continue. In return, children were also expected to take care of their parents in their old age. This of course is no longer widely prevalent as children are pursuing their interests all over the world and it is not practical anymore to carry out one's traditional duties in the traditional way.

When it comes to a Family Business, in the pre-1990s monopolistic, non-competitive, black market economics that prevailed in India, sons automatically joined or succeeded their fathers in Zamindari-style family businesses. If there were four sons, all the four could join and jointly do the work even though just one of them could have done the whole job! Those were easy days of joint families with businesses prospering in a shortage economy. Daughters were still out of bounds as far as business or business succession was concerned.

In those days, 'nepotism' as we understand today was a meaningless concept as it was a practised way of life in families in business.

In multi-family family businesses today, practising nepotism can be bad for business unless you are the only business in the world selling gold, or even toothpaste, or namkeens, or masks, or rubber bands. In business, a family business or otherwise, we are only as good as our results. Therefore, nepotism is bad if you are deliberately compromising on business performance and results that obviously happens when your son or daughter does not have the required professional competence to successfully manage the family business.

In a multi-family business, there can be attempts at nepotism by more than one family. If they are competing for the one available position, it is an opportunity for conflict since there will be a winner and a loser. And if the loser was obviously of a higher competence level, and the business performance slips, the conflict can spread, become more complex, and finally threaten the future of the family business. A family business must commit to medium and long-term profitable business growth in everybody's interest through professional merit-based management and governance.

It will be cheaper to keep an incompetent relative – who must be accommodated for family reasons – away from a position he does not deserve by supporting him with a neutrally designated position away from direct involvement with the family business. In my experience, such situations are common and require bold solutions to protect the business from being threatened by incompetence.

Some advice to the younger generation: Do not compromise on the best education you can afford and opportunities to work outside the family business in a good organization in a competitive industry for at least five years. Interact and compete on-the-job with professional managers and people at different levels. Get some experience in marketing, during this time at least for a year – close interaction with customers can be a humbling experience. At the end of this period, I feel you will be well-rounded and confident and ready to take on leadership responsibilities in your family business. With your good education, and with the competitive work exposure outside your family business, you will not require nepotism to prop you up.

12

Succession

'Succession' as a process must not be translated into over-simplified nepotism or a whimsical exercise in which a dominant family member forces a wrong decision, deliberately overlooking merit, and the others must go along to maintain the peace. Combined with a lack of accountability for delivery of targeted performance, power and nepotism together form a lethal mix that prevents merit-based succession.

A good 'Succession Plan' will re-structure the enterprise to harness the leadership skills and potential of competent members of the family, and therefore help create new growth opportunities that will further enhance opportunities for the progress of other family members, and the family enterprise group.

Retirement-based Succession, or 'Letting Go', has become more complex today as older generations are fitter in their late sixties, and in their seventies, even while younger generations aspire for greater responsibilities in their thirties and forties.

In many cases, 'Letting Go' to ease 'Succession' can be facilitated by an attractive and productive Retirement Policy where the 'Elder' will continue to enjoy certain perks of higher management, but without direct and actual operational or strategic responsibility. Concurrently, the Retirement Policy must also support the elders' social and economic status in relevant social and business circles and community.

A challenge to merit and competence-based 'Succession' also comes from other young claimants who obviously lack the required qualifications but in terms of family relationships consider it their right to succeed in critical and powerful senior positions. Unfortunately, if the merit-less succeed, the failure of the Family Business is guaranteed. Ultimately, if no family member makes the grade, instead of making costly compromises, a family in business must have the courage to appoint a competent 'Professional' from outside the 'Family' to be the 'Successor'.

13

Advice to the Younger Generations of Family Businesses in India: I: If you do not become professional, the Family Business will enter a stagnation phase and find it difficult to survive.

1. In normal circumstances, traditionally and historically, the founders of family businesses and their sons and siblings tend to be close together, as in a Joint Family, and generally run the family business through informal understanding and respect to the elders in the family.

2. With the emergence of the younger generation, the numbers involved in the family business may increase and at the same time, the relationship between younger generation members may not be as strong as between members of the older generation. This could be because from childhood they may study in different schools and grow up with their own set of friends and so on. The older generation's sense of closeness is unlikely to continue.

3. Also, by the time the younger generations begin to manage the family business, and this has been particularly true in India from the 1990s, the business climate has become extremely competitive, along with the rise in the aspirations of employees and their expectations about career progression and rewards.

4. Therefore, with an increasing number of family members in business, and their aspirations for more wealth and better

lifestyles, the only solution to motivating qualified employees and beating the competition is to focus on continuous growth for which professional inputs are required.

5. Professional management of family businesses is also important because our markets today are both local and global. The aspiration of the family business must be to become a 'Local and Global Professional Enterprise Brand'.

6. This aspiration can only be realized when family business motivations and actions originate from the continuous renewal of commitment to the future, through medium and long term contextual strategic thinking, and on business goals to be achieved within defined periods.

7. Futuristic Strategic Thinking is not only about the existing businesses, but also about major diversification into new sectors....it is also about developing yourselves to be better entrepreneurial leaders to be able to meet the demands of today's markets, and today's employees, and multiplying knowledge requirements.

Therefore, *the future of your family business is inextricably linked with the professionalization of management thinking and action by the Family Members in Business (FMB).*

8. Let us now look at what professionalism in action means to the FMBs themselves:

    8.1. FMBs have 24x7 responsibility and accountability for the successful functioning and performance of the family business and all its constituents.

    8.2. FMBs should be available and accessible to each other in person 24x7 on a need-to-contact basis, even when on a vacation.

8.3. Management and Performance Competence, and Competitiveness, 24x7, are indispensable and necessary professional assets that an FMB must possess if he is aspiring for higher positions – and this requirement does not change even if you got pushed up with an element of nepotism.

8.4. The family members managing the family business should be in contact and discharge their responsibilities wherever they are in the world at whatever time to protect the interests of the family business.

8.5. FMBs should never make the excuse of not being able to do something because they are 'away from the office' – they are supposed to be in command of their resources, to get things done, even under the most difficult circumstances.

8.6. In today's world, you cannot be 'away' when you are needed most, because of the critical position that you hold.

8.7. An FMB – like a Professional Non-Family CEO – is answerable to the designated higher Executive Authority or Board or Committee on his plans and performance.

8.8. Even if the CEO/Head is an FMB, and a brother or a cousin, he is answerable to the designated Executive Authority, as above, and the Executive Authority needs to evaluate his performance, on behalf of the stakeholders in the family business.

8.9. The FMB who is a CEO/Head cannot regard himself as the sole owner of the Company/Division of the family business of which he is CEO. You are all owners of the company/division, in proportion to the stake-holdings of each family in the family business. You all have a stake in the Company's/Division's performance, and therefore in the CEO's performance.

8.10. The FMB CEO/Head has been nominated by the family stakeholders, to protect the family's business interests, and not because he is the sole owner of the company or division.

8.11. If you find it difficult to question a CEO/Head because he is an FMB, it is advisable to appoint professional non-family CEOs who can be held accountable for their performance, without fear of family sensitivities.

9. *You as a family member in business, occupying an important position, can escape responsibility and accountability, only if you are willing to give up the management responsibility you hold, and just want to be a 'Promoter-Owner-Investor'*. Till then, you are 100% accountable, because of the professional management position you hold, and the accompanying status, salary, and benefits from it.

10. If you can understand and 'live' the difference between 'ownership' and 'management', you are beginning to understand 'professionalism'.

11. Just putting in the hours will not do – you need to be visionary, inspiring, and motivate great performance all around, and get off the beaten path. There are no limits on what you can achieve...

12. As far as the professionals who work for you are concerned, they will be watching you closely, and tune themselves to your work culture, and eventually, you will get the professionals you deserve. You have to be excellent in the way you conduct yourself, on and off work, in your depth of relevant knowledge, your appreciation and encouragement of others'

knowledge and contribution, and your willingness to learn, and be performance oriented, to attract the best to want to work with you.

13. Facing a moment of truth today can fuel the future with new aspirations and competitive energy....and consequently, ongoing positives for the present and future generations of your family business. The moment of truth includes critical questions you need to ask yourself:

   13.1. What is the value-add in terms of real growth, after providing for inflation and price increases?

   13.2. Is it possible for you to define with some clarity, the profile of your family business group, in terms of each business, and the expanded responsibility of each FMB in charge of the business, five years from now?

   13.3. For each one of you, what is the future all about? What are you going to build?

   13.4. Will you have developed the leadership qualities to attract and bring on board an elite professional team and have the management capability to make them deliver as per your Business Group's vision and aspirations?

   13.5. Will you have made the family business attractive enough for future generations?

   13.6. Is your 'life's mission' threatened by what is expected of you? What is your life's mission?

   13.7. *Are you aware that you have the freedom to live the way you want, but, you do not have the freedom to depreciate what you have been entrusted with, to protect, and to grow?*

14. **Finally, Remember that opportunities....**

    14.1. Are infinite

    14.2. You must look for them – they will not come to you

    14.3. You must look at the world as your market

    14.4. You must create time for identifying new opportunities, not for work. There will be people to do the work for you.

    14.5. Remember, falling business growth erodes both wealth and confidence.

    14.6. Stagnation breeds conflict breeds distrust.

    14.7. Conflict tends to multiply rapidly, with and without reason.

    14.8. Negative emotions overtake reason, prevent damage control, and everyone loses, now and into the future.

15. **So, what makes a Family Business successful?**

    15.1. History?

    15.2. Designations?

    15.3. Salary? Perks?

    15.4. Power to order people around?

    15.5. Mutual independence?

    15.6. Physical presence?

    15.7. Freedom to withdraw money?

    15.8. Freedom to spend?

    15.9. Luxury vacations?

15.10. Knowledge?

15.11. Qualifications?

15.12. Awards?

15.13. Profile?

15.14. Personality?

15.15. Connections?

16. The answer is: None of the above. In the absence of PERFORMANCE, they are just 'Data' and 'Cost' and 'Unhealthy fat' that can destroy a business from within.

17. The family spirit is at its highest when results are good, and there is cash flowing all around…for all stakeholders…and for growth.

18. Finally, ask yourself this fundamental question, to decide whether you are a winner or a loser:

Should inheritance boost the capacity to achieve,
or
should inheritance give you the right to be complacent?

14

Advice to the Younger Generations of Family Business in India on Professionalization: II: Client Experience: *A senior, long-serving non-family manager's letter to the new Younger Generation Directors...*

"Forgive me today for not addressing you as *Sir* (maybe from tomorrow I will call you, *Sir*). This is because today I am writing to you not as an employee but as a well-wisher, as an elderly person and also, as a teacher of Management.

At the outset, let me once again congratulate you all for assuming full-fledged responsibility as Directors of the PluDor empire. It is a great achievement but also a heavy responsibility to shoulder. I spoke a few words yesterday but because I had become emotional, I could not complete what I wanted to say. Today I want to share some of my thoughts, some sweet some not so sweet.

I belong to a community where business is never discussed, while for you, business is in your genes. And hence, obviously, I will not speak about business. But I will speak on a few aspects of its management. I still remember a statement by a respected Senior Director when we bought a new manufacturing unit in 2006/07: "Jiten, you are a good employee but not a good businessman!"

I belong to the old school of thought and so do your parents who built this empire called PluDor, literally from scratch. Have you ever analyzed or wondered what is it that worked for them so favourably in their pursuit of success but did not work for many more of their contemporary businessmen? Was it luck, or was it magic, or was it more than all this?

Let me mention only some of the strengths of the promoters which I have observed so closely over the last twenty years. The reason for me to speak about this is because no management school will be able to teach what these thoughts can teach. They are raw, ground level, and time-tested thoughts:

1. First, sheer hard work and a strong belief and confidence in pursuing success. I have heard a lot many stories about their struggles in the initial years. By the time I met them, they had already achieved much and built a name. But I have seen hard work in another aspect while travelling with them in the US and England: the number of meetings they held, the number of people they met, and the number of notes they made. Hats off to them!

2. Their business acumen that helped them both to identify, and create opportunities ahead of others, and grab them with both hands.

3. Their capability to select the right professionals as their subordinates and colleagues and to sustain them for decades. They treated senior employees like me with great respect, and never as subordinates. I do not remember a single day in the last twenty years when I have heard them use abusive language. They would express their displeasure but without hurting anyone. They are great Team Builders.

4. The concept of employee-inclusive 'Family' or *'Parivar'* were not mere words but a genuine expression of their desire and visible in practice.

5. Sometimes their concern went beyond an employee to his family. Like mine. Any time they met me, they have first asked

about my son's progress or the health of my wife. Someone may call this a mere HR trick, but for me, it was the extended family concept in its true sense and practice.

6. Their understanding of the business was thorough, both in technical and in commercial aspects.

7. My appetite to compete and progress became strong, obviously to earn more, grow, and stay ahead.

8. Humanitarian concern: When we were forced to stop our activities at our new location, for an unavoidable compliance reason, not a single employee was asked to leave. Nor a single month went where salaries were not paid before the fifth of the month. Which management will have this concern in today's world? People could have been offered two or three months' salary and asked to leave legally. But no. Our promoters sustained all the financial pain and allowed employees like us to continue without disturbance. Probably in business terms, they were unprofessionally foolish, but for us, they symbolized nothing less than Gods. I do not know whether the word "magnanimous" is right to describe this. I salute them for this.

9. This analysis will not end because of my respect and love towards them. Not that everything was good or went the right way. Neither do I say they did not commit errors. But instead of pinpointing these, in the next paragraph, I am going to talk about some of the challenges and requirements which we had to face and address.

10. When you voluntarily accepted the revenue target of Rs. 2500 Million, I will describe it as 'resolve', or 'strong desire to achieve'. Whenever we make such a resolve, we must bow to God and to parents and to teachers. So, let us bow first. The moment you bow to someone, it helps to reduce both ego as well as pressure.

11. Next, let us accept this as an achievable target and not merely a dream. This is where your generation differs from the promoters. Not only are you targeting big, but you also have the confidence and the desire to achieve the same.

12. But do you have the right people in the right place? You might have inherited the company from your parents but is it essential that you should inherit their teams also? I think in the next two to three years you should build your own teams. It does not mean you should get rid of oldies like us, but it is advisable to create a good combination of youth and experience. 'Youth' to match your speed, and 'experience' to restrain and to guide the team to move in the right direction. This will bring about 'integration'. I was tempted to ask all the managers gathered yesterday as to how many of them have the capability to be in the new team to meet tough future challenges. I am sure half of them would not have the capability required.

13. How do you sustain performing employees? This is the toughest challenge you will need to address. To some extent the promoter generation was lucky. In the sense, they built their teams in a less competitive situation.

14. Today, the ability to retain an employee is not only part of HR's function. It is far higher than that. In our generation, the employees in PluDor did not grow as fast as the company grew or as fast as their friends in other industries grew. Yet, this difference was not sufficient to tempt a departure. However, the expectations of present generation employees are far higher with increasing competitive opportunities. You will now have to work hard to ensure career and monetary growth opportunities across performing integrated teams.

15. We have to change the image of being a 'Family Promoted' company to being a 'Professionally Managed' company. Where and when do we start? Now, at this moment, and from ourselves. You have to understand that today's professional employee prefers working for a 'company' rather than for an 'individual'.

16. I sometimes ponder the question: Did PluDor attain its full growth potential in the last ten years? Unfortunately, the answer is negative. Your team has to answer this question and overcome hurdles to deliver on targets. Like a production manager gives tens of excuses for not meeting capacities, we, managers, always found excuses for not achieving what the company was capable of. A positive work culture is required without delay – like a good production manager who will analyze bottlenecks and downtime and will correct himself and the team at the earliest, to beat targets.

17. The promoters are individually different. Their individual priorities are different, their styles are different, their approach is different, everything is different. But they have cohesion. They complement and supplement each other and hence could succeed. You will have to make a special effort to 'rise above self' to achieve this cohesion. Expecting this from present youth is difficult but not impossible.

18. There was a slide on the screen yesterday. It said something like "A Goal without a Plan is a waste…" This has been a drawback in PluDor in the past. *We dreamed a lot, we talked a lot, but we planned the least.* You understand what I'm referring to: the use of technology for production and business. No modern company can meet today's delivery speeds with tight margins without modern technology. In the last three or four years, we have started using technology in

the real sense. We need to exploit technology both at offices and on shopfloors to attain higher operations and delivery speeds at the least cost.

19. An active long term HR Policy with a career development orientation and good work environment is absolutely indispensable for you to succeed today.

This will go on and on. But if you have really liked this lengthy mail, I appreciate your patience with me. Truly, there is a lot more for me to say, but this is enough for today."

15

Advice to the Younger Generations of Family Business in India on Professionalization: III: Client Experience: Your chance to prove that you are Entrepreneurial Leaders, and not just MBs (*Maalik-ke-Bete*/Children of the Owners): Revised Performance/Growth Budgets/Targets/Business Plan of each Division of PluDor for the next three years to start with…

1. The younger generation of the PluDor Family now has the sole responsibility for executing the profitable growth of PluDor and its divisions. The trust that the elders and the Executive Committee have placed on you was based on your confident assertion that in fact if you are allowed professional independence to manage your divisions, you can deliver much better performance than was promised in the earlier business plan.

2. You have now been given the chance to translate your confidence into action. And being part of the promoter families of PluDor, you will be expected to be entrepreneurial leaders with the skills and commitment to deliver a performance superior to what non-family professional CEOs can deliver.

3. The time has come to prove your real worth:

    3.1. Are you entrepreneurial leaders, or are you just MBs?

3.2. Do you think you can clearly reveal your potential as independent entrepreneurial leaders:

> 3.2.1. ...by the way you set out your revised budgets/plans/targets for executing the type of top line/bottom line and growth performance...
>
> 3.2.2. ...that will effectively prove that you are as good or better than your best-performing peers in the industry?

3.3. Anything less will not justify the confidence that your elders and the Executive Committee have placed in you.

4. The presentation you are going to make to the Family Council, must project :

> 4.1. Your professionalism: Your role henceforth is of accountable CEOs wholly in charge of delivering targeted performance, for the divisions and areas within your management control.
>
> 4.2. Because you are familiar with members of the Family Council does not mean you can take liberties on commitment to performance. Nothing should be taken for granted. All relevant issues, strategies, and solutions must be placed up front, on the slides.

5. Be honest, passionate, determined, comprehensive and visionary in your new approach through the presentation.

Please remember while preparing your presentation:

> 5.1. Real growth happens only if there is a net increase in the quantity manufactured and sold, less sales returns.
>
> 5.2. Real growth is also about increased coverage of old and new markets and the creation of new customers.

5.3. Real growth is also about creating new business through the introduction of new products and new applications of old products.

5.4. Real growth is NOT a value increase arising from short term gains/windfalls arising from adverse market/environmental issues faced by competition, like the issues faced by Chinese manufacturers.

5.5. Real growth is about accurate execution to translate plans into actual performance. Real growth is not about a good presentation of a business plan or budget, EXECUTION IS THE KEY... on budget....as per plan. Consistently, year after year...

5.6. Entrepreneurs cannot have the luxury of making excuses. The moment they get into 'Excuse Mode', they are no longer accountable CEOs or entrepreneurs. Then they are just plain maalik-ke-bete!

5.7. The enemy of execution is excuse, for non-performance against commitments made.

5.8. Execution is about having a Plan A/Plan B/Plan C always in place to realize business targets. Execution is not about inventing escape routes to '0' Growth, for lack of ideas.

I am also responsible for the radical change that has been brought about, and therefore have a strong self-interest in your success. The future of PluDor, the value of PluDor, and all that PluDor is connected to is in your hands. Your own career will now depend on how you can steer PluDor to a position of national and international recognition as a significant global player in your industry.

16

Advice to the Younger Generations of Family Business in India on Professionalization: IV: Client Experience: The Trivistral Group: Annual Retreat Exercise: "Questions that need answers…from the Fourth Generation…"

1. Starting last January, a 'Process of Change' was launched through the involvement of a professional external advisor to reinforce the desire of the Trivistral Business Family to continue to work together towards business growth, with a change in entrepreneurial outlook to cope with greater competition, as well as seek newer opportunities.

2. As part of the Process of Change, the management of the Group's businesses in the Equipment Distribution Sector were transferred in 'Succession' mode from the third to the fourth generation.

3. As part of the 'Succession' process, and to ensure maximum independence in decision-making for the fourth generation, the Executive Committee was set up with fourth-generation FMBs in full control, and with full freedom to plan and to direct the future of the Trivistral Group.

4. The primary questions that need to be answered today are: (4.1 to 4.8):

    4.1. Has the 'Process of Change' met its objectives? If the 'Process of Change' failed, where do we go from here?

4.2. Has the 'Process of Change' helped the Group move forward significantly in meeting its objectives? If the 'Process of Change' has helped to move forward significantly, then, what next?

4.3. Both, in case of 'failure' or in case of having significantly moved forward but could have been far better, what are the 'constraints' that the fourth generation FMBs face internally, within themselves, and within the larger Family Council, that has constricted or slowed down the 'Process of Change' from one of complacent routine to a more performance-oriented, professional work culture, with clear leadership and direction?

4.4. Does the fourth generation have the will, determination, aspiration, and foresight to ensure that the 100-year-old family enterprise will survive another century?

4.5. How? The first and second generations acquired and built assets that protected the third and fourth generations. The third generation conserved these assets and helped the Family Business hit a century. What will the fourth generation contribute similarly to the fifth and sixth generation – in terms of family business governance, in terms of family business management, in terms of family business growth and performance, and in terms of building and multiplying family business assets?

4.6. Do you have, or propose to have, a continuous process of communication, discussion, interaction to evolve and innovate short, medium, long term plans and strategies for action?

4.7. What is your expectation from the third generation in terms of encouraging you and assisting you in your pursuit of moving the Trivistral Group into a higher performance curve and work culture?

4.8. Will you, in this process, promote a culture of enterprise and achievement, by preventing the safety and security of inherited wealth from suppressing entrepreneurial aspirations and business leadership opportunities available to the Trivistral Group Family, over the next 100 years?

5. *Ask yourself this fundamental question:*

Should inheritance boost the capacity to achieve,
or
should inheritance give you the right to be complacent? Who wins in the end?

"WHEN YOU ARE IN CHARGE, YOUR JOB DESCRIPTION IS CLEAR, AND IT IS ALWAYS LARGER THAN WHAT YOU MAY HAVE ASSUMED. YOU CAN NEVER NOT HAVE TIME, YOU CAN NEVER NOT HAVE THINGS TO DISCUSS, YOU CAN NEVER NOT HAVE TIME TO LEAD, YOU CAN NEVER NOT HAVE TIME TO SUCCEED, YOU HAVE A CONTINUOUS OPPORTUNITY TO CREATE A PRODUCTIVE WAY OF FACING THE CHALLENGE OF THE PRESENT AND OF THE FUTURE, TO INSPIRE THE NEXT GENERATION, AND TO PERPETUATE A LARGER FAMILY BUSINESS RIDING INTO THE NEXT CENTURY. THERE ARE NO EXCUSES. THERE ARE ONLY OPPORTUNITIES."

17

Roadmap to Professionalization: The Starting Point: Exercise for Younger Generation Family CEO's Progress Appraisal (Not Started: 0/Outstanding: 10)

1. Continuously Planning/Setting/Executing/Meeting Performance Targets: Top Line and Bottom Line.

( )

2. Telescoping/overlapping Growth Plans on a minimum three-yearly basis.

( )

3. Performance priorities include attaining and maintaining a high level of Industry Competitiveness and Industry Leadership.

( )

4. Achieving Shareholder and Market Acceptance of Growth and Performance leading to continuous appreciation in Market Capitalization.

( )

5. Key Managers accountable for clear Performance Targets for their respective responsibilities/functional areas/departments.

( )

6. Zero Defect Manufacturing and Work Processes.

( )

7. Zero Waste Manufacturing and Work Processes.

( )

8. Timely and Effective Compliance to Legal and Statutory Obligations that wins the respect of Government Departments/Personnel.

( )

9. HR plus HRD to ensure Training, Career Development, Promotional Avenues for retention of key employees.

( )

10. Clean, Green, Safe, Hygienic, Disciplined Employee Friendly but Demanding Work Environment.

( )

11. Clean, Green, Healthy, Nature-friendly Aesthetically Designed External Landscaped Environment.

( )

12. Customer Friendly, Visitor Friendly Entry Gate Security and Office Reception.

( )

Raju Swamy/PROMAG//Family Council/27-02-2021

18

My answers, based on Indian experience, at the Q & A Sessions of the FBAW (Family Business in the Arab World) Conference (Virtual) November 04-05, 2020…(The conference was sponsored by The American University, Sharjah, and by Tharawat Magazine for Family Business)

1. How can Next Gen initiate conversations with the older generation on succession without causing offence, as mortality is a tricky issue?

   The very fact that family business issues are now discussed transparently and professionally, as in this FBAW Conference, means that if growth and continuity of the family business are important, one cannot treat 'succession' as a sensitive issue.

   Succession through death in the family is a reality. The sooner founders and elders put family members at ease on the discussion of this issue, the more secure will be the business.

   At some point, a founder or elder must convert himself or herself into a 'patriarch' who always has the best interests of the family at heart, in feeling and in action.

2. What is the best strategy to keep the family business growing strong for years, while we know that there will be obstacles from the management because of differences in vision, education, etc., between different generations in the family?

The best strategy to keep the family business strong in the long term is to focus on GROWTH. Please remember that without exception, the core logic of family business is that "Growth Unites, Stagnation Kills".

A family in business will be at peace only if the family business is successfully managed to grow continuously and help the 'family' multiply its wealth and resources.

It is important to have competent FMBs manage a business to make this happen. Family members who claim equality and rights but have little or no competence must be supported in style with adequate resources on condition that they stay away from the family business totally and permanently. It will be cheaper to keep incompetence in check by paying for it than to induct incompetent members of the family into the management of the family business and risk its destruction.

3. **What is the solution to the problem of different ways of thinking between the founder and the new generation in the family business?**

A genuine founder of a family business will always see the new generation as fresh 'potential for growth' requiring direction, freedom, and encouragement.

If he admires himself as the epitome of perfection, and the rest of the family as mere dependents, the family business has no future.

A good founder should respect the future, have confidence in the younger generation, and should know when to let go.

The next generation should design a fair and attractive 'retirement policy' and a respectable designation for the founder so that he hands over with dignity and without diminishing his status in society.

4. **How to keep the values of the family business alive across generations?**

   4.1. A non-controversial transparent past.

   4.2. Success as a business both financially, and in terms of reputation with employees, customers, suppliers, and with regulatory and facilitating institutions.

   4.3. Identifiable values

   4.4. Strong brand.

   4.5. Adaptability to the future with growth potential for both traditional and modern mix of diversified businesses.

   4.6. Stable family relationships over a significant period.

   4.7. Identifiable individual personal professional and wealth earning potential with recognizable merit recognition systems.

   4.8. Timely 'letting go' by senior generations in line with a good retirement policy.

   4.9. Only the competent among the family must be allowed to manage the family business, with a lean structure. Less competent claimants to management positions should be taken care of/supported outside the family business brand.

   4.10. A strong, disciplined, and functioning Family Council is indispensable to protect the evolved values that have ensured the consistent and sustained application of the above-defined conditions of perpetuating the family business.

4.11. A Family Constitution will be an added asset and an affirmation of faith in themselves, for such a family business, as a record of values already sustained by the family/families owning the family business, over past generations.

4.12. If a family business has managed to survive with success, reputation, and brand intact for at least three generations, possibilities of multi-generational participation as above become feasible.

19

The Logic of Business is to Maximize Profit... Within a defined and necessary Value-based Operating System...

The Values that a Family in Business has with a history and heritage to be proud of, must continue to understand and translate into action:

We have to make a success of our business, in perpetuity, while enforcing and observing the following beliefs:

1. *We will not shortchange our Customers.*
2. *We will not shortchange our Suppliers.*
3. *We will not shortchange our Employees.*
4. *We will not shortchange our Shareholders.*
5. *We will not shortchange our Family.*
6. *We will not shortchange our Country.*

When we make a loss, we shortchange everybody. And, the moment we think we are helpless, we are no longer 'in business'. We do not deserve to be in business, any more, for we have obviously lost the will to learn, to innovate, to grow...

In a Family Business, always: Growth Unites, Stagnation Kills.

20

Entrepreneur CEO Performance Self-Appraisal for Business Success

Daily/Weekly/Monthly/Quarterly/Yearly

This 21-point checklist summarizes the minimum strategic objectives of an Entrepreneur or of an Entrepreneurial Manager against which performance is to be appraised based on the management principles of LEAN Manufacturing and of TQM. This checklist can be adapted to any type of business, including non-manufacturing, as it is primarily related to *Maximizing Management Quality and Productivity to ensure Business and Organization Success.*

1	Maximize information generation to 100	
2	Minimize cost to 0	
3	Minimize inputs to 0	
4	Eliminate defects to 0	
5	Eliminate rejections to 0	
6	Eliminate waste to 0	
7	Maximize quality to 100	
8	Maximize innovation to 100	
9	Maximize knowledge to 100	
10	Maximize market awareness to 100	
11	Maximize forecasting to 100	
12	Minimize "Time to Market" to 0	
13	Minimize "Decision to Action Time" to 0	

Continued...

14	Maximize External Customer Satisfaction to 100	
15	Maximize Internal Customer Satisfaction to 100	
16	Maximize Employee Satisfaction to 100	
17	Maximize Output to 100	
18	Maximize Performance to 100	
19	Maximize Value Addition to 100	
20	Maximize Stakeholder Value to 100	
21	Maximize Brand Equity to 100	

Qualifier: As of now it is a simple self-appraisal exercise on how an Entrepreneur-CEO has scored against the 'Ideal' (Maximum/Minimum). It is an attempt at understanding the 360-degree management accountability of an Entrepreneur – CEO. The exercise can be extended to allow for the 'ideal', the target commitment for a specific period against the "ideal', and actual achievement against the target. This just means adding two more columns. It is really designed as an honest and simple appraisal for self-motivation, rather than an article or handout.

Overall, assessment is a somewhat dangerous exercise because 'averaging' will tend to cover-up serious deficiencies. The CEO needs to use this process to set his priorities clear for improving his leadership performance. It could be interpreted as a continuous focused SWOT Analysis.

21

Warning Signs in a Family Business

1. Lack of structured and timely communication, even on important business matters.

2. No 'Formal Accountable Business and Performance Planning' that can maximize contribution based on the number of family members directly involved in the management of the business.

3. Nepotism can be a major obstruction to delivering accountable results as nobody can question anybody on performance when multiple generations are 'directors' functioning in a relatively 'free-for-all and no questions asked' business environment.

4. Lack of clarity on 'who is accountable for what': a very loose management structure.

5. If any of the above is true to any degree, then the 'growth' requirement of the company and of the partner-families and directors is not being met and conflicts will arise from possible business stagnation.

6. Even in older family businesses with a decent history and profile, many aspects of management of the business may be good, but not enough in terms of overall business growth in line with the number of family members directly managing the family business.

7. Resolution of the above issues, if they exist, is an absolute must for productive and profitable survival, growth, and perpetuation of the family business.

8. If none of the above holds good for your family business… Congratulations.

22

TIERRRA©

TIERRRA©
TRUST
INTEGRITY
ETHICS
RELATIONSHIPS
REPUTATION
RESULTS
ACCOUNTABILITY
CORE VALUES FOR A FAMILY BUSINESS

Copyright © 2018 Raju Swamy/ PROMAG Consultancy Services/ April 13, 2015
All Rights Reserved

23

TIERRRA© Explained – Values and Professionalism in Family Business

1. Values based on TIERRRA©

1.1. When we talk of values in the context of a Family Business, the most obvious variables that instantly come to mind are: trust, integrity, and ethics.

1.2 However, irrespective of good moral standards, the key to peace, prosperity, and perpetuation of a Family Business is the successful pursuit of the business itself.

1.3. Therefore, values include 'delivering positive results' as proof of accepting one's accountability for achieving business performance.

1.4. Results derived from performance are a critical practicable 'value' as important as the moral or personal human quality variables that enrich and strengthen relationships.

1.5. The powerful practice of values, both through superior human qualities and through outstanding business results automatically enhances reputation.

1.6. The interconnection and interdependence – in TIERRRA – between Trust, Integrity, Ethics, Relationships, Reputation, Results, and Accountability are obvious tools of success of a Family Business in perpetuity.

2. 'Professionalism' flowing from TIERRRA©

2.1. When a Family Business makes serious moves in line with TIERRRA, it also automatically moves towards becoming 'Professional'.

2.2. Becoming 'Professional' is when 'Values' are not about preaching, pretension, and position, but about delivering visible business success through business and management practices that are sustainable across the Family, across Stakeholders, Markets, and Customers.

2.3. Business and Management Practices include Developmental Leadership, Business and Strategic Planning, People Development, People Career Progression, Innovation across the board, and any related business, organization, and market positives.

2.4. TIERRRA makes a Family Business indestructible, from the inside and the outside…

(Copyright © 2018 Raju Swamy/Founder & Advisor to Family Business/PROMAG Consultancy Services/Bangalore INDIA - 560004/Email: rajupromag@hotmail.com/ Cell: +91-9845271498/www.promagconsult.in)

24

Values and Professionalism in Family Business: What is the SOP to get Goddess Lakshmi's blessings to be successful in business?

The Chairman of a more than a century old Indian traditional family in business asked me to explain 'professionalism' in the context of their business culture. He said that they were God-fearing practicing Hindus, worked extremely hard and looked after their employees well. They also paid their taxes.

I respect all religions because finally, they are about learning, respecting, and practising values. In answering the Chairman, I decided on experimenting with my more familiar Hindu religious logic:

1. The most important and frequent prayer occasions among Hindus, and in the business community, are the ones to Goddess Lakshmi as in Lakshmi Puja or Lakshmi Pujan. Goddess Lakshmi because she is the Goddess of Money and Wealth.

2. It is also true that not everybody is successful in getting Goddess Lakshmi's attention to the extent desired. Why?

3. Many of us may not be aware that there is some homework you must do before you go to Goddess Lakshmi. We can also imagine this homework as 'Standard Operating Procedure' – SOP for short.

4. Going straight to Goddess Lakshmi is like taking a shortcut… let me tell you a story: There was a small but ambitious vendor in a small town who was extremely frustrated with his lack of progress, despite working hard. Finally, not having an answer, he approached the village astrologer. The astrologer studied his horoscope, his palm, and his forehead and said confidently that he had a good future and was even likely to win a lottery.

   The vendor was happy and resumed his trade. As time passed, he noticed no change – he found he was where he was, and blamed his plight on the astrologer. The now angry young man came to the astrologer and accused him of cheating, lying, and so on. The astrologer quietly asked him "Did you buy a lottery ticket?" That is where the angry young vendor had gone wrong…he had not done his 'homework'. It is simple, you must first buy a lottery ticket to stand the chance of winning a lottery – how can you assume any outcome without doing your basic homework?

5. Indian Religious Logic for Success in Business, as I understand or interpret it, is quite simple: You must do your homework before you can approach Goddess Lakshmi, for favours. Let me explain 'homework' in the present context:

   5.1. Ganesh Ji is the 'gateway to solutions'…You need to attempt to enter your Business Highway with Ganesh Ji's blessings.

   5.2. When the gate opens, Lord Ram must be prayed to and assured about your commitment to practice good governance and good management, prior to driving on the Business Highway.

   5.3. Since the Business Highway is long and arduous, and the end is never in sight, you must pray to

Lord Krishna, the ultimate Strategic Advisor and Mentor, to show you the easiest way to travel the Business Highway. Lord Krishna has designed for you a series of multiple-choice tests and information that will help you overcome obstacles provided you are able to understand and interpret weather conditions, road signs, markers, emergency numbers, locations of workshops and re-fuelling stations, and of restaurants, to ensure an uninterrupted, safe, and smooth drive on the Business Highway, to reach your planned destination.

5.4. It must be understood that getting an A or an A-Plus is extremely difficult in Lord Krishna's tests as most of us are in a hurry and lack the patience to minutely examine all the information in small print that you assume to be routine. One can enter the Business Highway with a B or B-Plus…of course, Lord Krishna will be totally aware of what will happen to you since he is aware of your destiny, and what you deserve.

5.5. Therefore, most of us, with B+ or even an A, discover that the Business Highway itself is not smooth… there are rough surfaces, potholes, oncoming traffic, stray animals, thieves, and careless people that you were unaware of since you were in a hurry to answer questions and did not read the small print in Lord Krishna's multiple-choice tests. The small print in fact was the guide to discover the strategy to manage and govern the rough road to your destination. Now you will understand why it took Lord Krishna a long time to convince Arjuna in the Bhagawad Gita to choose the right path…and it is taking even longer – centuries – for even the holiest of our holy pandits and teachers to be able to claim full understanding of the ultimate in strategic knowledge and advice, followed by precision in execution that led to the victory of the Pandavas.

5.6. Now that you finally understand how extraordinarily little you know about efficiently driving on the Business Highway, you realize your ignorance, and your need for more knowledge, and education…you will now have to approach Goddess Saraswathi, the Goddess of Knowledge and Learning.

5.7. It is only after paying your respects most appropriately to Goddess Saraswathi, by requesting her blessings to imbibe knowledge, through education and training, and by spending time to acquire that knowledge, can you even think of approaching and praying to Goddess Lakshmi. Goddess Saraswathi has designed Knowledge to be Infinite, with no limits to acquisition, so be humble in your claims of having acquired knowledge when you approach Lakshmi Mata Ji.

5.8. Goddess Lakshmi will not only look for proof of your following the SOP, but also check your evaluation reports and final grades from Ganesh Ji, Ram Ji, Krishan Ji, and Saraswathi Mata Ji.

5.9. Lakshmi Mata Ji will finally determine what you deserve and on the delivery logistics.

5.10. You can see, therefore, that the route to Lakshmi Ji is a long one, and there are no shortcuts. You must follow the Standard Operating Procedure (SOP) in Business to get Lakshmi Ji's attention. This SOP, to reach Lakshmi Ji for a successful outcome is 'professionalism'.

5.11. All the other Gods and Goddesses on the Hindu religious map are either support systems or regulatory bodies protecting you as you pursue your homework, guided by your values, as in TIERRRA. If you are really outstanding in your homework and deserving of her attention, Goddess Lakshmi Ji may even request Hanuman Ji to give you a lift up to heights not reached by others till now!

5.12. **And, finally, the 'Ultimate' conclusion. Lord Shiva and Lord Vishnu are Guardians of Creation ... Lord Shiva eliminates 'Waste' – as is recommended in 'Lean Manufacturing' – and Lord Vishnu creates 'Assets'. If Lakshmi Mata Ji gives your Family Business a positive grade, in proportion to that grade, Lord Vishnu perpetuates your Family Business. If Lakshmi Mata Ji gives you a negative grade, Lord Shiva will rid the Earth of your presence. History – including current history – has many examples of both disappearance and of multiplication.**

5.13. Real Profitable Power comes, not from your designation, but from your homework: Governance, Strategy, Knowledge, Performance, and Results. From your Professionalism. And from your endless desire to seek, and to achieve ...**TIERRRA is the strongest Family Business Foundation of Professionalism you can have in your Family Business ... Wear it proudly and chase your VISION to Infinity ...**

25

The Family Council

What happens when hardworking, well-meaning father, sons, uncles, and cousins of an old family business are so busy managing their business for long hours every day that they hardly have time to meet? They find a lot of things going wrong and they do not know why...they all did manage to meet over lunch last week and all agreed that something had to be done...unfortunately, problems continued, and they just could not find time to sit together. And so, management-by-crisis and fire-fighting continues...and since they are also God-fearing, apart from hardworking, and generally good human beings...they must be enjoying some protection from "up there"! There can be no other explanation for their continued survival, on a tightrope going higher and longer.

Sitting together over a hurried breakfast or lunch or dinner and discussing issues at random and not having time to finish a conversation does not constitute a problem-solving business meeting.

A 92-year-old family business, being managed by the third generation of partners, brothers, and cousins, all nice and honest people, was also the oldest distributor of over 50 years for a premium product of one of India's most reputed Mumbai-based business houses. The Marketing Director of the business house arrived suddenly one morning, met the eldest brother of the family business, and insisted that all the family managers get-together for a meeting with him. Such a 'meeting together' was rare and not normal in this family business. Anyway, the meeting started, and the GM asked them whether they knew how many bills were pending for payment to them, and what was the total outstanding…there was total silence…none of the partners were aware of the situation having become serious. The Mumbai Business House withdrew the distribution rights and from then on it was too late to set matters right in the family business without getting into a destructive blame game. The family business has ceased to exist. When the founder and his son ran the business, it was a household name in the large state it operated in.

Extreme examples are necessary sometimes to drive home the seriousness of a culture issue – when survival itself comes into doubt.

Informal meetings do help in varying degrees, but they are generally incomplete, with a random start and a random end, and with no record and no accountability.

Let us consider a reputed family business with enlightened management. The family directors and managers do meet occasionally, or when there is a major business decision to be taken, or when there is an emergency. Here again, the meeting is held with a broad unwritten agenda, or some messages may have been shared in advance. The problem here is that without a formal agenda, no fixed time duration, and, sometimes, with family members floating in and out, and, of course, calls being taken, and with liberal and frequent serving of tea and light snacks…people are serious, but in an informal easy-going and casual ambience, the quality of decisions and input to output productivity will be below par.

Let us consider a family business with multi-generational issues, problems of conflict over holding positions of power, or disputes of various kinds, or over-lapping management responsibilities… impossible to have problem-solving meetings.

The common thread across these examples is the lack of communication across the Family Management Structure. Organized, structured, formal, accountable communication is non-existent. Everybody is equal. Who will dare to take the initiative? Peaceful non-decision making is better than aggressive debates over right and wrong. Under such circumstances, the management productivity of the FMBs is low and most definitely will affect the performance of the entire business.

It is normal in multi-divisional organizations to have at any one time maybe ten important issues requiring solutions or decisions. If these ten issues are formally scheduled for discussion in a management meeting and if somebody is coordinating and setting up the meeting, with a date, time, and agenda, and prompting discussion and resolution within the meeting, it is realistic to assume that enough effort will go into helping take the right decisions. In the absence of such coordination, in a free-for-all informal meeting, one will be lucky even if half the issues get discussed over double the time spent.

This is where the Family Council comes in. The Family Council is the first concrete step towards the professionalization of a family business. The priority of the Family Council is to ensure profitable performance and growth of the family business. For this to happen, the Family Council, consisting only of all family members actively involved in the operations and management of the family business, accept that peace and well-being of a family, or of families, in a family business is primarily dependent on the family business performing well on all parameters that contribute to Profitable Growth year on year. For the family business to perform well on all parameters of success, every FMB must ensure meeting of the required performance targets for the functions he or she is responsible for. When they accept that they must meet performance targets, they become accountable. When they become accountable, they begin to realize they are dependent on others also to meet their respective targets…and in this process, a unity of purpose comes into being with the Family Council being unanimously accepted as the special purpose vehicle they will all ride on together to reach their chosen destination.

Yes, I agree. The process of forming and making a success of the Family Council is not as easy as it is made out to be. The success of the Family Council depends on **not** hiding any issue of conflict or difference of opinion under the carpet to maintain artificial peace. The success of the Family Council also does not depend on the regularity of meetings and full attendance of all concerned. The success of the Family Council depends 100 per cent only on making the family business achieve continuous and profitable growth in the medium and long term. And simultaneously create an enduring Business and Product Brand that builds great value for the families involved and for all other stakeholders in the business.

Every Family Council Meeting – at least once a month – must have an agenda and must have follow-up action. There will have to be a self-motivated Chairperson, perhaps by rotation on an annual basis, or even longer. No Non-Family Member will be part of the Family Council or be present even to take notes, write minutes, etc…This is to enable discussion and sharing of views without reservation by Family Council Members.

When the constituents of the Family Council accept the seriousness of their objective, and the benefits that consequently flow to them, a whole lot of weaknesses in the family business like nepotism and conflict of interest, will diminish and disappear over time. The process of professionalization of the family business becomes stronger, faster, and permanent.

For me, as a Family Business Advisor, with every new client, once the familiarization and problem identification phases are completed, the transformation exercise always starts with the acceptance and formation of the Family Council. The Family Council is about positive communication to build a legacy of business and family success lasting many generations.

26

Client Experience: Melsons Group: Family Council: Meeting Checklist

1. **Primary Business Objectives:**

    1.1. **Business and Management Performance:** To ensure that the businesses where the family has management control and a controlling financial interest contribute to the wealth and well-being of the family in perpetuity through:

    1.1.1. Quality, Stability, and Growth of Human Resources employed in the Businesses.

    1.1.2. Knowledge, Networking, and Alertness to be able to adapt with innovation and productivity, in time, to changing markets and to the changes in the larger business environment.

    1.1.3. Continuous Growth both in Financials and in Market Expansion that will generate increasing management and employment opportunity, and dividend income, for the family.

    1.1.4. Continuous and Sustainable Growth that will reflect positively to the relevant external world and which will result in an increasing valuation of the companies that will in turn contribute to the building of wealth of the Family.

1.1.5. Sustained Growth and Performance of the Group Companies over time, to be used to develop a Group Brand Equity that in turn will attract external investment for expansion and for new ventures.

1.1.6. Group Brand Equity will also help to attract competent senior professionals who are essential for sustained growth.

2. **Career and Succession Planning:**

    2.1. Identification of Leadership Positions that will require successors in 3/5/7 years.

    2.2. Identification/mapping of career routing over 3/5/7 years of next-generation Human Resources from within the family to execute a Plan of Succession including training for domain expertise and leadership.

    2.3. Identify Leadership Positions where, for want of appropriate human resources from within the family, external qualified professionals have to be inducted, or where such professionals from within can be identified and trained to higher levels of leadership.

3. **Retirement Planning**

    3.1. Who will retire when?

    3.2. Phase in/Phase out Plan

    3.3. Financial Security

    3.4. Social Security

    3.5. Family Support.

4. **Continuity and Performance of Not-for-Profits/Charities.**

5. **Agenda for Monthly Meetings:** The agenda for each meeting will have to flow naturally from the checklist, and include:

    5.1. Regular Performance Reporting from the family's perspective: For each company, for each charity institution.

    5.2. Each Next-Gen professional from the family to make a focused presentation on an area in the business that requires attention with a fresh perspective.

    5.3. Other agenda listings will consist of priority attention areas for that month from the Primary Objectives Checklist.

6. **Meeting Format:** Formal seating/Professional Family Meeting/Performance and Solution Driven/*A Chairperson from within the family, by rotation, including Next-Gen members of the family.*

Organization, Minutes and Follow-up: A family member to take up this formal, accountable, leadership responsibility for the productive success of each Monthly Meeting, for a specified period.

27

Client Experience: Functions of the Family Council of the Trachmas Group

1. The Family Council is not a statutory board but an overseeing strategic governance institution created by the Promoter Family to be the 'guardian angel' of all that constitutes the Trachmas Group as of today, and in the future – in terms of performance, growth, and sustainability:

    1.1. The Investor/Promoter Family

    1.2. The Shareholders

    1.3. The Enterprises, their assets, and their people

    1.4. The Relevant Community within which the enterprises operate, and beyond, through institutions delivering health, education, and other services that will benefit the community

    1.5. Compliance with the laws and regulations of local administration, and of the State and Central Governments.

    1.6. Promoting and sustaining the values of the Trachmas Group in action across the Trachmas Group Community including the family and including employees and associates and affiliates forming part of the business enterprises and the non-business, not-for-profit social and educational Institutions.

2. To be able to play the above role effectively, **the members of the Family Council will have to be Company-Neutral and Employee-Neutral.** Their vision, their wisdom, their experience, their stake, and their accountability will be to the 'Trachmas Group' of which all entities defined above are a part.

3. Consequently, the **members of the Family Council will also be accountable to themselves for specific areas of Group Management, to drive goals, and to review performance and progress, at each Family Council Meeting.** Each member of the Family Council should take charge of one or more of the following Group Management Areas for continuous reviews and improvement:

   3.1. Group Financials/Business Plan

   3.2. Group Projects/Technology/Expansion/Diversification

   3.3. Mission to move up the Value Chain

   3.4. Management Quality, and Development of the Trachmas Group Management Cadre

   3.5. Group HR Strategy

   3.6. Senior Management Recruitment: Subject to approval by the Family Council

   3.7. Group Brand Promotion and Development

   3.8. **Minutes of the Family Council Meetings and follow-through Action**

4. External Advisors may be inducted into the Family Council as 'special invitees' only after the family members reach an advanced degree of comfort and effectiveness to function as a strong and united professional family business team. 'Special invitees' will only be invited to specific meetings where their inputs are deemed necessary.

28

Family Constitution – 1 – Introductory

From my experience with family business clients, I can broadly list the sequence of events that make developing a Family Constitution inevitable:

1. In a traditional first-generation, joint-family managed, single-location family business, with a founder-patriarch in control, and unmarried dependents, and where everyone meets everyone else constantly, at home and at work, with high mutual visibility, contact, and constant communication, un-challengeable rules of business flowing down from the patriarch, oral or written, guide the vision, direction, and management structure of the FMBs. The patriarch is the living 'Family Constitution'.

2. Extending this further, the culture of 'respect for elders' and falling in line with their advice on any subject under the sun helps preserve family peace and unity.

3. At this stage, 'father plus unmarried sons' is a peaceful, cooperative 'single family' community.

4. When sons get married, we have a multi-family business as each 'son plus wife' becomes a separate unit, though within the same household. Still, the patriarch will rule and manage peace and unity, through the ups and downs of business, as failure or success is jointly shared by everyone. However, there are hidden tensions as the new wives feel stifled in a single-kitchen restricted environment. These tensions do

get passed on to the husbands, but they manage to carry on without disturbing the relatively calm waters.

5. Then come the third-generation babies and increase the responsibility of the second-generation wives and simultaneously create an atmosphere of multiple independent families with clear self-interest about their respective well-being, now and in the future. The joint family set-up cramps the freedom the daughters-in-law seek to run an independent household and have more influence on their husbands. The wife's discomfort begins to seep into the psyche of each husband and begins to impact their 'brotherly' working relationship – the seeds of conflict are planted. This phenomenon is something I have observed first hand with a client family and influenced a change.

6. Even in the best of families, if the performance of the family business is good and there is growth, and upwardly affordable lifestyle changes begin to happen, conflicts can be kept in check and 'work' is managed with a mutual desire to avoid breakdowns in business. The father – the patriarch – continues to be a major influence, but the going gets tough for him. Till now, the management structure has been more informal with duplication of responsibilities, loose job descriptions, and a total absence of accountability for results. Fortunately, basic family characteristics, professional competence, and value systems are good, and this mix ensures a method in the madness.

7. Soon, the sons themselves realize that their 'method in madness' management structure and style has too many holes and beyond a point, they are finding it difficult to attract good professionals or even to retain the ones they have. Confusion in leadership and direction is beginning to show. Performance, growth, and market reputation are threatened.

8. The most significant weaknesses of a traditionally structured family business are:

   8.1. When family members must be accommodated in the family business because they assume it is their right, and there are no rules of entry, the equivalent of a single job or responsibility is shared loosely by sometimes two and even three family members. For the equivalent of three jobs, there can be eight family members. Productivity per head is non-existent, nobody is fully responsible for a task, nobody is accountable, and finally, nobody really knows what to do and they just live with the situation for money, perks, and privilege, supported by nepotism.

   8.2. Despite the glaring weaknesses of the poor contribution of individuals and structural confusion, if the business is doing reasonably well, nobody wants to disturb the family relationships and peace by asking questions. Issues are obviously pushed under the carpet if the 'money flow' is undisturbed.

   8.3. There has to be a breaking point to the over-stretched elastic… The family business now either starts winding down or, in a sudden flash of enlightenment, the survival instinct kicks in and triggers a serious attempt to change the 'free-for-all' business culture.

9. At this juncture, a 'Family Constitution' in some form is the solution to ensure a process of integrated wealth management, of ensuring minimum economic support, of protection from unforeseen disasters and calamities, and of providing personal and social security into old age.

29

Family Constitution: 2: Some Directions towards evolving a Family Constitution

There are no textbook definitions for a Family Constitution as the criticality of conditions to agree upon depends on the number of families and family members involved, whether listed companies or private limited or partnerships.

However, based on my experience with many family business categories, I am clear that a Family Constitution can be designed and sustained long term only if the families concerned have a desire to stay together. For them, a Family Constitution is a guide to being together productively in peace by following mutually acceptable conditions for profitable management of the family business.

At the same time, it is my finding that where within a family business the constituent families have been in conflict over wealth and property matters over a long period, and the issues continue to exist, a Family Constitution will not sustain.

Finally, a Family Constitution is of no use in a family business with poor management competence and where the Family business is either stagnating or underperforming over a long time.

A Family Constitution is not a magic wand.

A Family Constitution must normally include the following minimum headings:

1. Ownership Holdings and Structure
2. Family Business Group's Vision and Values
3. Governance Code as per values of the family business and as per Company Law Regulations.
4. Family Council: Constituents and Functions
5. Performance and Growth Plans and Objectives
6. Terms/Conditions/Systems for induction of new family members into the family business, Degree of Autonomy, Reporting, Allocation of Management Responsibility, and Accountability for producing desired results, and the Rewards for fulfilling/exceeding pre-set goals.
7. Career Development/Professional Training
8. Succession Planning and Execution
9. Management Decision Making at Company/Divisional Level and at Group Level
10. Investment Decisions on Existing Businesses and on New Business/New Projects
11. Funding Norms: External/Internal
12. Risk Analysis and Protection
13. Remuneration and Performance Incentives and Rewards
14. Dividend Policy
15. Retirement Policy including Post-Retirement Remuneration/Pension/Post-Retirement Non-Executive Responsibilities and Official Status and Role
16. Resolving Differences/Preventing Conflict/Preventing Conflict of Interest

17. Corporate Social Responsibility (CSR)

18. Any other considerations/areas of agreement

In a family business with multiple families, multiple generations, multiple family members, multiple companies, and multiple locations, it is advisable to have a comprehensive, legalized, unambiguous, enforceable Family Constitution.

30

Family Constitution: 3: Note to a Client on ground rules, specific to questions that came up in discussions with them…

We are now on the threshold of a great new beginning where you have absolutely nothing to lose since mutual understanding mixed with professionalism can only make you winners all the way.

Based on some questions raised by some of you, the framing of a Family Constitution requires an understanding of certain 'ground rules' and supporting policy and procedures to provide solid shape to family members' relationships with the business and with one another as investors, owners, managers, and employees. This will promote sensible discussion, reduce arguments, and increase predictability:

1. The business must be acknowledged and respected as the source of the family's financial security. Though obvious, this is especially important because family members who do not work in the business, or contribute fairly to it, but share the fruits from it, may not understand the business's importance to the family's overall welfare.

2. Any qualified family member may apply for a specific job in the existing business or propose a new business. The keywords here are "qualified" and "specific." From the moment that a family start-up grows enough to make employing additional family members feasible, it should be well-understood that

just walking in the door and expecting a place to sit and get a cheque every month is not acceptable.

3. Similarly, proposing a new business entails responsibilities and accountability on the part of a family member without which the family is not duty-bound to support the venture, risking the resources of the entire family. However, when a young family member insists that he wants to take off on his own with a new project, and his proposal has some credibility, tell him to get independent evaluation and acceptance for consideration of loan or investment by reputed third parties, including leading banks and financial institutions. Based on a positive outcome, a decision may be taken to assist with part contribution…and establish this rule for the family business to take care of similar demands from others.

4. Family members who are designated to assume professional managerial responsibilities must be pre-qualified for the position or undergo the desired professional preparation that may include managerial as well as technical training. Family members cannot assume 'qualification and capability' just by being members of the family.

5. The need for health and growth of the business must override feelings of family relationships as only a successful business will contribute to the well-being of a family and its togetherness in business. This ground rule will also apply in the case of planning family ownership continuity and succession that qualification, experience, and preparation are essential.

6. The Family Constitution can also provide for the setting up of a multi-family 'Family Office' funded through defined annual or periodical contributions by partner-investor family members gainfully employed in the family business

and which can also be used to provide/enhance wealth and financial security for each of the investing families, in ways that can be defined specifically, including covering old age, medical insurance, education, emergencies, celebrations, etc.

7. The Family Office funds will be managed through a Group Family Office – to be defined in the Family Constitution.

31

Family Constitution: 4: Client Experience: Paramdhanam Enterprises: Content Guidelines for discussion and integration

Part I: The Fundamentals

1. **Mission Statement:** Converging on a common approach to business and its perpetuation as a single successful group entity. A checklist for consideration:

    1.1. Frequently Occurring Issues and Solutions

    1.2. Reflect the future and not the past: time perspective of 5 to 10 years

    1.2.1. Increasingly competitive business environment

    1.2.2. The prospects of the current business

    1.2.3. The need for diversification and its direction

    1.2.4. The need for professionalization of management and human resource development

    1.2.5. The need to convert past strengths into sustainable competitive advantages in the future.

2. **Group Business Objective:** Subsidiary to the Mission Statement listing specific targets for business growth, business development, and organizational change goals for implementation in the short term of 3 to 5 years. Some leading questions:

2.1. Where does the existing business stand in relation to the apparent maturity/decline stage of the generic product in terms of available and viable number of years in the product life cycle?

2.2. What can be the likely growth path for the Group under existing conditions?

2.3. What will be the required growth path, with and without diversification?

2.4. Financing options for growth: it is possible that the priority of family members may be on personal asset building for the benefit of their respective families relative to re-investment into the business. Acceptable options, including a mix of options, need to be identified.

2.5. Brand building: Group and individual companies

3. **The Formal Organization:**

   3.1. Clearly identified Profit Centres, areas of responsibility, authority, and accountability for each business-active family member subject to Quarterly and Annual Performance Reviews.

   3.2. The effective establishment of the Group Executive Committee and the Corporate Organization Structure.

   3.3. The entry level of the next generation of family members, allocation of business roles, their induction, development and monitoring: structure and process.

4. **Governance and Conduct Code:** A set of principles of management and of conduct that will support the Group's Mission and business objectives. The following is an 'essentials' (though not exhaustive) checklist:

   4.1. A shift from informal to formal decision making.

4.2. Process of professional decision making and acceptance of decisions.

4.3. Transparency in relation to business role and responsibility.

4.4. Information sharing.

4.5. Values and discipline.

4.6. Professional qualification, experience, capacity, and potential to determine entry into the business, business role and business role-related reward system of partners, and of promotion to higher responsibilities.

4.7. Performance Appraisal

4.8. A clear distinction between 'business-active partners' and 'dormant' partners in the application of financial benefits (and liabilities) arising from the business.

4.9. The 'Public Face of Partners' to be defined in terms of application to community service, public and private social institutions, government institutions and departments, and other similar bodies.

4.10. Corporate image and lifestyle parameters to be defined: not necessarily to be interpreted as restrictive.

4.11. Inter-personal relationships of partners and its reflection in the business role.

4.12. 'Mutually dependent as well as mutually exclusive': Norms for a productive relationship between the business and the families.

Part II: Specific Policy and Procedures Issues

1. Induction norms and process of induction for next-generation family members.

2. Career Planning and Management Development for family members.

3. Human Resource Development (employees).

4. Financing business and growth: future options.

5. Retirement of a family member from 'business active' status due to old age/health/other justifiable reasons.

6. 'Opting out' of partnership: the 'settlement' norms and process.

7. Performance Appraisal against accountability norms.

8. Remuneration package and performance-related reward system for 'business-active' partners in addition to normal profit-sharing of the partnership applicable also to 'non-active' partners.

9. Relocation of partners in India or overseas, arising from business improvement and growth needs.

10. Minimum professional norms for qualifying as a 'business-active' partner, subject to availability of a viable professional vacancy.

11. Norms for female members of partner families to enter the business, as partners or as employees, provided they qualify on 'minimum professional norms'.

12. Creation of a 'Nest Fund'/Mutual Benefit Fund or similar Trust and other organized means of providing for financial protection to families of partners under specified circumstances.

32

A Note on 'Conflict of Interest' for purposes of Shareholders' Agreement/Family Constitution

1. It is an accepted fact in the family business domain that individual stakeholders in a joint multiple family promoted family business may also have their respective private businesses that were already in existence before the launch of the joint family business.

2. It is also an accepted fact that as a progressive accumulation of wealth takes place among the individual family stakeholders, they may promote or aspire to promote their own respective private businesses.

3. However, it must be understood without ambiguity by every stakeholder concerned who also has interests in a private business or businesses that the most important qualifiers or conditions for the peaceful and profitable and sustainable perpetuation of the joint family business are:

    3.1. Agreeing to and enforcing a 'non-compete' clause between the joint family business and the private businesses.

    3.2. Agreeing to and enforcing a clause or clauses that will eliminate or avoid 'conflict of interest' between the joint family business and the private businesses in areas including but not restricted to Brand, Time, Expenses, People, Products, Markets (Territories, Channels, Customers, etc.).

3.3. Defining fair 'Time Distribution' between the joint family business and one's private company is important to retain confidence and performance effectiveness of key professionals in the joint family business, both in terms of motivation and of delivering targeted results.

3.4. Where the conflict of interest is serious but unavoidable, the merger of the concerned divisions of private companies with the joint family business may also be considered as a solution provided there is mutual benefit.

3.5. It will be a serious mistake, or misunderstanding, to assume that incorporating 'non-compete' and 'avoidance of conflict of interest' clauses can be enforced by informal understanding to avoid individual family sensitivities. The peaceful, profitable and united transition of a multi-family family business even to the second generation will be at risk if a formal agreement is not arrived at and enforced.

3.6. At the same time, it is also to the advantage of the stakeholder families, that they have the freedom to arrive at a mutually satisfactory agreement taking care of all their respective interests.

3.7. *Therefore, settle on an unambiguous Policy Agreement on avoiding Conflict of Interest, duly accepted, and signed by all members of the Family Council of the joint multi-family business. This 'Policy Agreement' can also be a clause in the Family Constitution.*

33

Client Experience (1999): Pioneer Natural Products Ltd.: Perpetuating a successful Family Business: Strength and Progress Analysis and Recommended Action

Objective: To sustain and perpetuate the exceptional achievements to date in terms of productive assets, brand equity, market share, industry leadership, and corporate and family reputation for integrity in business, in customer relationships, and in service to the community.

1. The Founder and his older sons converted a 'Nature-based mass consumption product' (NMCP) from a commodity to an FMCG brand with sustained long term investment in product development, supplier development, production, logistics, marketing and customer relations.

2. Established competitive advantage and industry leadership consequent to brand-building, product and packaging innovation, and domestic and international distribution logistics. productive assets, brand equity, market share, industry leadership, corporate and family reputation for integrity in business, in customer relationships, and in service to the community.

3. Family values instilled by the Founder of the business reinforced by the succeeding generation.

4. The Business Vision of the family reflected in the continuity of success in business results and in wealth creation, simultaneously with the enhancement in reputation for integrity in business in the eyes of business associates, of customers and of the public at large.

5. Financial discipline has not only influenced the success of the entire business process but has also reinforced the importance of family values in sustaining business success.

6. Promoted a corporate culture that reflected a powerful and positive combination of family values, business vision, and financial discipline, sustained by a cooperative business leadership style, practising restraint yet without sacrificing results.

7. Other contributing factors to success:

   7.1. Business and financial discipline strengthened from experience of humble beginnings to determination to establish leadership by example.

   7.2. Close-knit, single (large) family aware of humble beginnings and united in purpose.

   7.3. It is often true that in a closely held Family Business, whenever the partners get a chance to sit together, intentionally, or otherwise, formally, or informally, a Board Meeting can be said to have taken place.

   7.4. It is also true that if the partners are few and have grown up together from the 'log cabin to White House' stages of the development of the business, and if the business has achieved continuous success over a significant period, there is almost total unanimity on matters concerning the management of the business.

7.5. Differences, if any, are again contained within acceptable limits in the larger interest.

7.6. The process of partnership is also made easier by the partners being brothers from the same family. And in the Indian context, respect for family hierarchy also assists the process.

8. **THE CHALLENGE OF THE FUTURE: To bring about change as a pre-emptive exercise, in a radically changing internal and external environment within which the business and the partnership operates, to preserve and perpetuate the 40 years of success, into the next century.**

9. Internal factors influencing change...

    9.1. Marriages. More families. More partners...

    9.2. Management by brothers of a single family to management by brothers and their respective children.

    9.3. Additional induction of working partners of the next generation implies the provision of appropriate management slots that do not cut into the management authority of the current generation who are as yet young enough to continue in operations and the policy-making structure for at least another five to ten years.

    9.4. Blending 'Great Expectations' to 'Proven Success'... Humbler origins, hard work, cautious dynamism, mutual understanding, and actual achievement have to accommodate the attitudes of a younger generation with a prosperous upbringing, modern international education, high expectations and aspirations, and restlessness to 'move on'.

9.5. This fusion must take place in line with the Group's underlying vision and management culture which has generated wealth and reputation for the benefit of the business and the family over the last forty years.

9.6. Inevitable dilution of informal decision making... with the increase in the number of operating partners, of different generations, and from multiple families, and with the induction of more professionals, the informality of 'breakfast board meetings" may be hard to sustain.

9.7. The attitudes of partners themselves may undergo subtle changes over time as they advance in age, and as their responsibilities for their respective families increase, and as their families further extend. Self-interest may predominate.

9.8. Retirement, or even 'opting out"... A partner may wish to retire, in the normal course, due to ill health or on account of old age. In a closely held business, how is retirement to be interpreted? What must be built into a Retirement Plan to preserve the economic status quo of the retired partner and his interests. Are options possible? Can a formal 'Retirement Age' be relevant in the future context with attendant benefits?

9.9. Will there be a specific business or related role for a retired partner who has been active in the business?

9.10. A partner may wish to opt-out of the business. A formal 'Settlement Process' needs to be defined.

10. **Profit Centres, Performance, Accountability...** In the emerging competitive scenario, within and outside, how is the 'deviant' performance of a partner to be dealt

with? Performance would need to be defined in terms of functional responsibilities, profit centres, budgets, results and accountability.

11. **Interlinked will be the need to establish clarity of roles and role relationships among partners in the business.** How is a good performance to be rewarded or recognized among the 'business-active' partners?

    11.1. New 'entrepreneurs', new opportunities... The NMCP business has since inception been the main support of the Group and its partners. However, being nature-based and labour intensive, and in terms of competition from the 'unorganized sector', there may not be adequate opportunity for accommodating more 'entrepreneur partners' into the family's core business.

    11.2. With limited opportunities in the NMCP business for the emerging entrepreneur partners, diversification for growth becomes imperative.

    11.3. Relocation of Partners... As the Group business grows, and with increased global opportunities, with matching capabilities being available within the families, it may become necessary to station partners in locations beyond their current major location, even abroad.

    11.4. Entry criteria for a 'Business Active' partner... Do partners, by virtue of their being members of the promoter families of the business, become automatically eligible to enter the Group business or to take on functional responsibilities irrespective of them possessing business, professional or specialist qualifications and/or experience that will add value to the business of the Group? Will 'family succession' automatically mean rights to 'management succession'?

11.5. Recognizing the difference between 'business-active' and 'dormant' (or 'non-working') partners: The business-active partner has the right to be appropriately remunerated, rewarded and recognized for active contribution to the business on the job, in addition to profit-sharing, as distinct from a 'non-working partner' being entitled to profit-sharing only, with no role in operational and functional decision making.

11.6. Gender freedom...to enter the business... If there are qualified spouses, daughters/daughters-in-law, can they enter the business? Under what conditions?

11.7. Formal, Accountable....and together? Removing apparent contradictions between the evolution of a 'formalized' management process and structure as against continuing to perpetuate 'family togetherness' in business between the partners.

11.8. Families, long term security, and 'togetherness'... Providing long term security to families of partners to face any eventuality: Creation of a Nest Fund or appropriate Trust with a continuous flow of adequate resources and norms for management and disbursement. Taking care of long-term security could strengthen 'togetherness' without compromising on the formalized competence-based management structure.

11.9. Upgrading employees' capacity to deliver...The need for increased competitiveness and for growth also demands upgrading of employee quality and capabilities to deliver results. A certain degree of traditional 'paternalism' has so far meant 'compromise on poor performance so as not to hurt'.

11.10. Human Resource Development, Training, and Employee Relations will need to be formalized into the change process in line with meeting the demands of competition of both products and people.

12. External factors influencing change....

12.1. Taking care to restructure the organization to adjust to internal changes, adequately and in time, strengthens it to counter external changes which can be relatively easy to forecast, like competition, product substitution, environmental restrictions and laws, obsolescence, higher costs, lower margins, labour laws, militancy, technology, new product options/applications/markets, global opportunities.

12.2. There can also be unforeseen external events motivated by government policy, natural calamities, international events, etc...

12.3. The future is, therefore, a 'melting pot' of a significant 'generation mix' of increase in numbers of operational partners, of increase in the number of families involved with a more complex association of interests, attitudes, and aspirations, growing competition, complexity and costs of doing business, greater functional autonomy with accountability for results, lesser mutual visibility on a day-to-day basis with the consequent possibility of communication gaps...

12.4. The 'future' also indicates the emergence of increased complexity of inter-partner relationships in business with consequential fallout on the management of the total business process, with far-reaching implications on business results.

12.5. In analyzing emerging complexities, it must always be remembered that the NMCP business is the 'cash cow' of the Group – the motivation for demand for the product is based on sentiment, superstition, tradition and habit, variables that can sustain generic demand long into the future.

12.6. To have attained industry and market leadership in a product that is apparently easy to manufacture, imitate, substitute, etc., is undoubtedly because of sustained management and marketing capabilities proved in the field by the Founder of the Group and the second generation partners.

12.7. A note of caution…It is difficult to imagine any other product or industry that the Group has diversified into, or will have to diversify into, providing the type of stability, returns, growth and reputation that the NMCP business has given to the Group and the family. It is the 'cash cow' that will continue to enable and fuel new investments and growth – in the process of restructuring for change consequent to the induction of the third generation into business operations.

12.8. The protection of the 'cash cow', therefore, becomes almost a sacred duty of all partners when the contents of the 'melting pot' must be re-moulded to the relevance of a changed situation.

13. **Restructure... and 'reinforce' consensus...** The 'Restructuring' operation, because of the natural evolution of an illustrious family, must be handled with care, by the strength of mutual consensus that has held together so far and achieved remarkable success over the last forty years. But with one vital difference. Informal consensus must give way to a process of formalization of the consensus process, moving towards the professionalization of the interaction of partners directly involved in business operations.

   13.1. **The Starting Point...** Having considered the factors influencing change, and the inevitability of it, a good starting point is for the partners to decide by consensus as to what constitutes 'professionalization' for the Pioneer Natural Products Group (PNP Group) and accordingly evolve a Family Constitution, within the principles of the Group's objective (and philosophy): "to sustain and perpetuate the exceptional achievements to date in terms of productive assets, brand equity, market share, industry leadership, and corporate and family reputation for integrity in business, and in customer relationships, and in service to the community."

   13.2. **Prerequisites for a Family Constitution...** Partners must agree that there is a need to 'professionalize' the partnership 'on the job' to accept a new organization structure, functional responsibility, and accountability.

   13.3. Accordingly, this would mean the acceptance a clear demarcation between partners' mutual commitments to The PNP Group in their 'business-active' roles and commitments to their families as 'stakeholders' in the business.

13.4. To reinforce acceptance across the stakeholder families that 'formalizing' the business process and organization is to increase its long-term sustainability, to be able to provide for, to promote, and to always protect the families themselves in terms of their well-being and security and under all circumstances.

13.5. To instil in the third generation of potential 'business-active' partners the necessity to appreciate and consequently protect the achievements of the last forty years while adding value to the Group through their international exposure and education.

13.6. **Functional Role:** Formalizing the business role as a partner in-charge of a specific Operational Function in terms of: Responsibility and Job Definition, Authority and Accountability and Reporting, and subject to a mutually agreed Performance Appraisal and Reward System.

13.7. The Family Constitution will also cover the Functional Remuneration Package, Partnership Entitlement, Post-Retirement Financial Support, Family Security, Corporate Life-Style Parameters, Social and Community Service Contribution, Business Travel Entitlements, 'Non-Partner' Family Member Support System, and other mutually acceptable parameters.

13.8. **The Family Constitution…**Will emerge by consensus only after each internal factor influencing the change process has been matched with a solution and/or agreement.

14. **The Governance Code (to be included in the Family Constitution)**

    14.1. The Governance Code includes agreement on Information Sharing, Functional Reporting, Mutual Consulting prior to taking a decision on critical areas irrespective of functional responsibility, Consensus and Compromise to protect and promote Group interest, Idea Generation for continuous improvement to meet the sustainable growth and profit objectives particularly in the areas of Technology, Product Development, Business and Market Development, and Human Resource Management.

    14.2. The Governance Code includes assistance to individual partners, once they have entered the business, to professionally develop to their maximum potential: through mentoring, through functional rotation, through delegation, and through constant exposure to domestic and global trends in innovation and in achieving competitiveness.

    14.3. The Governance Code includes supporting each working partner with a professional career development plan that will at each phase of his career, reinforce his potential to contribute. This will include recognition of exceptional performance, upgrading of responsibility and consequent accountability, and encouragement to pursue professional training and development to continuously upgrade management capability.

    14.4. The Governance Code will provide for horizontal and upward mobility within the professional working partnership hierarchy in terms of responsibility, authority, accountability, and reward, and based on operational performance, on contribution to wealth creation, and on the ability to sustain and further the Group's business and community objectives.

14.5. In summary, the **'Governance Code', as a part of the Family Constitution, is to provide a strong commitment and mutual professional support in pursuit of the Group's objective, "to preserve and perpetuate, through personal example, the PNP Group's objective to sustain and perpetuate the exceptional achievements to date in terms of brand equity, market share, industry leadership, and corporate and family reputation for integrity in business, and in customer relationships, and in service to the community".**

14.6. Depending on the requirements of the constituents of a Family Business, a Family Constitution can be in a Legal Format in terms of details of constituents, and expressions to be used in each clause to rule out the ambiguity of interpretation. Also, a legal document is more binding than a non-legal agreement depending purely on the moral commitment of the constituents to the clauses agreed upon.

34

Client Experience: National Retail Partners Ltd.: A peaceful solution to a uniquely sensitive issue

This is something that happened in a successful Family Business many years ago, before the management shifted to the third and fourth generations.

The Founder started a traditional business involving door-to-door and street-corner sales. The product was relatively simple, made at home, and supervised by the Founder's wife. A very hardworking couple and business partners. They produced many children – sons, and daughters. The business also progressed.

Over time, the sons were educated and brought into the business. The elder sons came in at the 'struggle' stage and learned the business the hard way. The daughters helped the mother run the house and the large family. The elder children were brought up by the mother, in a simple lifestyle, and, as she grew busier helping her husband improve the business, the younger sons were brought up by the older daughters, but with a better lifestyle.

The elder sons had to work with their hands, owned bicycles, and later two-wheelers. The younger sons came into revolving chairs and tables and started with two-wheelers, followed by cars soon after. The younger sons had not experienced the struggle.

As time passed, it became slowly apparent that the Family Business was over-crowded with aspiring sons, and there were two mismatching cultures within the family. Also, the Family Business Brand had been built by the elder sons, and their feeling of ownership towards it was strong. Their market relationships and hold on the market were exceptionally good. International markets were beginning to be explored. And the elder sons were still young enough and hungry to do a lot more.

The younger sons felt under-employed. They hankered for the power and resources the elders had control of, legitimately.

Meanwhile, the Family Business was growing extremely well, and creating and multiplying family and individual wealth. So, money was not the issue here. There was also mutual financial integrity.

The fusion of old and young had still to happen. A brave decision was required, without rocking the boat.

Finally, by mutual agreement, and with friendly professional advice, the Family Business was split into two. The elder sons continued to manage the original Family Business, and a new Family Business with a similar product and market brands and strengths was born with the younger sons in control.

A lot of water has flown down the Ganga since then…maybe there will a sequel at a later stage.

The lesson, however, is clear: Run the Family Business well. Maintain mutual trust in money and wealth within the family, and within the Family Business. Bold, and sometimes difficult decisions are more easily made, in mutual business and personal interests, when integrity of family members in business is beyond doubt.

35

Client Experience: Gyanji & Sons: A 92-year-old Family Business destroyed by the Third Generation...

Gyanji & Sons was founded in 1901 with personalized shop-to-shop selling of textiles and grew soon into a business establishment trading in premium national brands of textiles, household and office steel furniture and security equipment.

The Family Business progressed and grew both in reputation and size, till about the late 1960s, with the management having passed on to the founder's son in the mid-1940s. During this period, Gyanji & Sons. achieved success both in business and reputation and became a household business brand in the state, with branches in major towns. In the course of time, from the mid-1950s onwards, the third-generation of sons got inducted and the business passed on wholly to the third generation – grandsons of the founder – by about 1960, with the passing away of the founder's son.

The grandsons of the founder, six members of the third generation, excellent human beings at a one-to-one level, were conventionally educated. With time, their lack of business acumen and discipline across the board combined with directionless, complacent leadership from the elder brothers began to show up in business performance and financials. As their families grew and personal financial needs increased, cash withdrawals by the partners followed no logic, and it is clear in hindsight that withdrawals were being made from resources that included tax dues to the Government, dues to suppliers, and dues against bank loans.

Two significant developments that stand out during these chaotic times were the loss of sole dealership for the premium steel equipment brand and ignorance and loss of control on inventory and overdue payments to principal suppliers. This resulted in the senior management of their principal suppliers coming down and issuing an ultimatum. It was clear during these meetings that none of the partners were even aware of the seriousness of the issues involved, including the numbers.

Even at this stage, there was little awakening, with none of the partners showing any real initiative to salvage the business. The inevitable happened. And even as the Family Business entered its last stages, the brothers (partners) worried more about the sharing of spoils in the event of the business collapsing, rather than having any regrets for being responsible for the death of a 92-year-old business institution. Today, in 2021, the family business, had it survived, would have been 121 years old, and in a radically changed business environment, full of opportunity.

Almost at the last stages, when there was still a small chance for a turnaround, one of the partners took the initiative to invite me to look at the issues. Even earlier, since I knew the family well, at various stages of my professional progress, I had drawn their attention – informally – to what I believed to be critical issues that needed to be corrected. However, nothing seemed to bother them as long as there was money in the cash box, irrespective of where it came from or where it was meant to go. Ignorance was bliss, till the very end.

To me, having consulted with family businesses for over 35 years, this experience with Gyanji & Sons is, unfortunately, relevant even today. Many family businesses continue to be troubled by problems of 'equality' overriding professional merit, rights overriding accountability, designation overriding performance, and short-sighted nepotism overriding visionary leadership.

This situation is worse in family businesses not growing fast enough to accommodate new family inductees who consider it their birthright to enter the business, and enjoy its pay and perks, irrespective of whether they have the desired capabilities, or whether an opportunity exists for them to contribute.

Client Experience: AsiaticChem: Avoiding the designation trap

"I am prompted to write this based on the imminent induction into your Indian operations of a few employees from the overseas subsidiary. I also suggest that there should be a Management Policy on Designations: both at the Corporate and Operational levels."

A few years ago, the CMD of a client company of mine was extremely keen, in fact, determined and desperate, to recruit a particular candidate for a senior technical position. This candidate was just the right fit to fulfil a critical need then. The interview went very well, except for one issue: the candidate was insisting on a designation that rationally could not be conceded to within the present organizational structure. The candidate was adamant, and the CMD was desperate: an extremely negative transactional situation to be in. The CMD gave in and in his frustration, almost shouted: "You can have any designation you want but you will do exactly what I want you to do!"

We are confronted by similar situations many times, and invariably take a short-cut position of 'resolving the problem when it arises', or 'we will cross the bridge when we come to it'. In this case, two critical managers threatened to resign – one left taking along with him two of his assistants, the other had to be 'bought' back.

My advice:

1. Plan well in advance for such induction, as well as for other future inductions.
2. Don't overload the structure to 'accommodate'.
3. Don't create compromises: designations are elastic and if they are pulled beyond the actual job content, they break, or boomerang, and can hurt.
4. Designations should truly match job content and supervisory boundaries.
5. Designations should not be thrown about as a reward, or a motivator, without back-up content.
6. Designations should not be created under threat.
7. Designations should support the structure, not structure support designations.
8. Be aware of all consequences before you take an insensitive decision, aimed at meeting a narrow objective.
9. Do not create too many designations. Instead, establish attractive multi-stage salary package structures per designation for performing employees, till they reach a stage where a vacancy exists either because of a promotion chain, or because of an exit, or because of expansion.
10. Don't make designations 'cheap'.
11. At Senior and Middle levels, it is better for the Family Council to take a joint, well-considered decision in the Group's interest.

37

Client Experience: Conflict resolution must also result in performance improvement: Progress Report to the Statutory Board of Prevexcol Exports Ltd. on my ongoing assignment with the Promoter Family

As we are hopefully entering the 'mutually positive last mile' phase of **Prevexcol Exports** in its present form and structure, I thought it fit, for the information of the Members of the Board, to summarize my work and experience with **Prevexcol:**

My role as a Family Business Consultant formally commenced when I met with the key promoters, Dr. Naveen and Suresh Kumar. The initiative for hiring me was Dr. Naveen's, and we had met several times before the formal meeting.

The fact that there was a conflict situation in the business did not bother me as that is part of the landscape that I usually deal with as a Family Business Consultant. However, in late October, when I met with the key managers of the company and when they presented their Business Plan for the year, I immediately discerned a state of extreme chaos.

Their Business Plan, already presented to the Board earlier, showed a performance target of Rs. 1100 Million for the year, backed by a strange organization chart with multiple crisscrossing lines tracking reporting, but with no clarity on individual responsibilities. When I asked them to explain the logic behind the target of Rs. 1100 Million, a big leap over their previous year's performance, and also explain who was responsible for making it happen, none of those present had a clue. They could not also explain how the organisational structure represented by the chart worked in practice.

After a couple of follow-through meetings and a better understanding of the magnitude of the management chaos, including the contribution and consequences of having the two key promoter-shareholders in a deep-rooted conflict, it was apparent to me that **Prevexcol** was a living but struggling and threatened business entity, and it had to be saved from collapse.

My view was also reinforced by the fact that even the Board Members had to contend with confusion and chaos in Board Meetings that seemed to perpetually end in a mess of mutual accusations and walk-outs, without professional discipline of any kind. The Board Members, being good personal friends of the promoters, were, understandably, helpless in such delicate circumstances.

The Monthly Family Business Board (FBB) – a version of the Family Council when there are just a few members – Meetings started effectively from December with Dr. Naveen, Suresh Kumar, Vilas (son of Suresh Kumar), and me at Dr. Naveen's residence and very soon thereafter at the company premises in the Industrial Estate. Since then, at least 64 FBB Meetings have been held, and I can accurately recall that conflict-induced disturbance has occurred only three times, yes, only thrice, making it 95% successful!

Even Board Meetings became more professional since my induction, with much fewer conflict-induced disturbances, and far more realistic and accurate presentations and constructive participation.

Coming back to my strategy, to start with, after detailed re-working of resources and competencies, the target for 2011/12 was revised to a more realistic Rs. 740 Million. With a continuous focus on performance and numbers, at three active Management Levels: FBB, MC (Management Committee) consisting of Promoters and Key Managers, and SPG (Strategic Planning Group) consisting of Key Managers and Departmental Heads, there has been steady growth, at a 'survival' level, finishing with a highly profitable Rs. 1280 Million in 2014/15.

Management stability, quality, and productivity have also been positive during this period. While the actual numbers have been achieved obviously by the Company Directors and Managers, they will also be the most competent people to comment on how I have contributed to this relatively positive trend, under the most challenging circumstances.

Also, during the period of my association, I have strictly avoided any conflict of interest in my association with either of the interested parties. At the same time, during this period, even they, Dr. Naveen, and Suresh Kumar, tried their best to be restrained at critical times to allow progress to the extent possible under the circumstances, of course of their own making! Our relationship has been cordial and professional.

The critical elements of conflict in family businesses concern Power, Money, Nepotism, and Space. Under normal conditions of continuous growth and creation of wealth, there will be enough to share equitably, and misunderstandings, if any, will be pushed under the carpet. The problem arises when there is stagnation, and squeezing of resources and wealth, then all types of questions, big and small, true, and false, will surface to make a misery of family relationships. **Prevexcol** is lucky that from chaos and near collapse it has survived and is now in a position to build a better future. I have played a significant part in this resurrection.

Today, we have entered what I sincerely wish is the 'mutually positive last mile': A Committee of the Board is working on a settlement between the promoters that will be mutually acceptable and will open fresher, significantly larger avenues for **Prevexcol** to operate with innovative products, on a scale more appropriate to be a recognizable force over the next 25 years, fuelled by a younger generation.

I am continuing my association with them over the 'mutually positive last mile' to help at critical moments. We cannot afford to let the 'mutually positive last mile' fail… it will be extremely unpleasant and expensive for the interested parties to recover from a failed effort…. and it may also spell the end of Prevexcol.

The Board of **Prevexcol** needs to rise to the occasion… I am with you.

38

Client Experience: Corporate HR Recommendations to Melsons Group: Priority Areas

The role of the Corporate Human Resources – also referred to as GROUP HR – is to develop and implement human resource management policies and strategies that will enable the Melsons Group to attract, recruit, develop, retain and sustain a high potential, qualified and performance-oriented Management Cadre to ensure succession, continuity, innovation, and positive growth of the Group Companies. This would include as a process:

1. Preparing a comprehensive data bank of all employees across the Group Companies in senior, middle, and supervisory positions.

2. Classifying them into A/B/C categories based on age, overall experience, and experience with Group, qualifications, domain expertise, track record, and growth potential.

3. Developing a career plan/map for each incumbent with lateral and upward movement within the organization, and formulating a Capacity Upgrading Plan incorporating Leadership and Domain Training Programmes, and Management and Process Exposure on-the-job with collaborators and other organizations.

4. When there is a gap between the position required to be filled, and the human resource available within, Corporate HR goes for fresh recruitment.

5. **Since key positions are based in a Tier 2 city, it is essential, as part of the recruitment process, to 'sell the location' to potential candidates in terms of both the professional's aspirations and of his/her family.** Particularly important are housing, employment for the spouse, education for children, an opportunity for extra-curricular pursuits for children and leisure activity for the family, medical assistance, security, and medium and long-term projections for the Tier 2 location from the family point of view. All this, over and above the employment position and monetary package. The location also has to be sold in terms of proximity to Chennai, and whether the Melsons Group provides guest house facilities at Chennai to specific levels of the management cadre on personal visits.

6. **Recruit/Induct Professional CEOs to head Group Companies.**

7. **Corporate HR in terms of the above will need to be driven by an FMB with a personal commitment to protecting the family's investment even as they move away from direct management roles.**

39

Client Experience: The Punjewal Group: A Family Business whose deep-rooted negatives drowned out the positives and prevented transformation

What follows is a real-life consulting experience of mine over an 18-month period where the Chairman of a fairly large Family Business consisting of multiple plants in multiple locations requested me to help them resolve business issues within the extended family – which consisted of ten family members, multiple generations, who were directly involved in the Family Business.

The significance of this case lies in the fact that both the Business Vision and the Family Values of the families in the business had little to do with business advancement and family reputation and more with settling inter-personal wealth and property disputes. The motivations of all key family members were questionable.

Ultimately, I had to withdraw. The three actual management reports plus a final letter will give you a clear idea of why this family business could not survive. There are clear lessons to be learnt here.

1. **The common behaviour and lifestyle characteristics of the Punjewal Business Family:**

    1.1. Zamindari *'ji huzoor'* management style of the 1950s/'60s/'70s with the classic 'Munimji' accounting practices:

1.1.1. The eldest brother, the family leader, in his early seventies, is the Chairman and is all-powerful, not just as the patriarch but wielding the power of a 'Super Zamindar' of days gone by.

1.1.2. Total and unquestioned control over money and family wealth is vested in the hands of the leader.

1.1.3. Money is used as a weapon of subjugation and loyalty, promoting politics and mutual distrust.

1.1.4. Money handouts are not necessarily for professional skills or for producing results.

1.1.5. In fact, easy handouts of money to maintain a disproportionate lifestyle killed initiative and incentive to practice professional business skills or to chase legitimate professional achievement.

1.1.6. More than half of the male members of employable age enjoy pay and perks but do not have full-time work, neither do they seem worried on that account.

1.1.7. All are unhappy and dissatisfied primarily because they want more money – in whatever form – for whatever they are doing or not doing.

2. **Not a single male member of the Family Business has a thought for the 'future'...in fact, they have no fresh ideas, no motivation, and no skills, to even debate sensibly on why the future is important for the Family Business and for all of them:**

2.1. Not a single male member of the family business is even concerned about the legitimacy of their earnings, in part or full, and feels extremely insecure if the status quo is threatened by change that would demand accountability and discipline.

2.1.1. As a reflection of the above, a senior member emotionally stated at one of the meetings when we were discussing the necessity for change: "We have worked really hard, day and night, and evaded taxes, and that is why we have these big houses and cars and our lifestyle, so how is change good for us?"

2.1.2. Similarly, a discussion of 'Values' at another meeting made people uncomfortable... not because they felt any guilt, but because of their fear that they may make less money if they ran their businesses legitimately!

2.1.3. Another young man – third generation – of the family business seriously described his ambition as "Today I am able to own an Audi and a BMW, and in a few years, I want to make enough money to buy a helicopter."

2.2. Many post-liberalization Indian entrepreneurs would have described their business aspirations in terms of building the world's biggest or best company in their respective product or service industry, or in building a "billion-dollar business" to be a business or market leader...obviously, to such people, achievement in terms of skills, size, quality, reputation is the core ambition to prove their leadership and business acumen and entrepreneurship...money is secondary and taken for granted as a by-product of business success. None of the male members of the Punjewal Products Group Family Business talk this language.

2.3 Nobody talks about management improvement or management strategies that are currently practised in progressive manufacturing companies. Practices like 'lean manufacturing' were unheard of.

2.4. There was little or no concern for the aesthetics and development of a green environment around and within their factories in multiple locations. Ironically, this is despite wanting an enhanced personal lifestyle for themselves as members of the Family Business.

2.5. The biggest and obvious weakness of the Punjewal Products Group today, with the existing management style, and aspirations, is the prospect of total disintegration because of stagnation and consequent breakdown of family relationships. Today, the bonds are already tending to be artificial than real because of the insecurities and distrust that the elder male members suffer from.

3. **Questions raised and solutions recommended in many meetings with the Chairman and FMBs directly involved in the family business:**

   3.1. Strong recommendation to discuss urgent critical issues confronting the Punjewal Products Group so that they move forward with a focus on resolving issues rather than discussing the same things again and again.

   3.2. The issue of the Group's business stagnation needs to be addressed as a matter of life and death for the Group's businesses, only then would they appreciate the seriousness of the situation they faced.

   3.3. Put idle family human resources to productive use.

3.4. Why have young men with MBA degrees not been utilized as per their education? Why were they sent to Management Schools and not encouraged to contribute to the family business – after the investment in their education and exposure abroad?

3.5. Why is there never a meeting/discussion/brainstorming on strategies to make the Group Companies grow significantly and profitably in terms of brand-building, in terms of marketing ideas and action, and in terms of new business development – to make products saleable with a good margin without having to resort to unethical means?

3.6. Why have they never thought of growth through 'forward integration' by adding value to their current product line as is usual with progressive family business groups? Even to consider this idea one would require intensive business and market knowledge, and networking within India and across the world, with possible large customers in the OEM space. The discussion on these issues was vague out of lack of interest and ignorance of facts.

3.7. Why do you always think that new projects will have to be financed internally, and therefore you keep saying 'there is no money'? Why not send the under-employed young people of the family into the wide world of business to come back with new ideas for attracting investment to grow either in your current fields or in radically new areas?

3.8. What benefit is it to the Family Business Group to keep whining, avoiding, postponing, keep talking the same things again and again, and keep doing things the same old way just because... because of what? Why?? What can be gained by aspiring for a modern lifestyle while the business stagnates with outdated management style??

3.9. Why don't you grow your existing companies by making the CEOs and other FMBs accountable for planned results with growth targets for both turnover and for profits, by identifying their KRAs and making them deliver on their promises?

3.10. Today, because you live and run your businesses as private, secretive, dictatorial small kingdoms – as safe havens which cannot be professionally questioned on performance and growth, every FMB suffers from tunnel vision and believes that whatever they do is perfect. So every meeting becomes a shouting match when there is even a feeble attempt at questioning something.

3.11. What you should be concentrating on are the questions I have raised, for your own survival, as a Family Business and as a family.

3.12. Believe me, if you do not act with Focus, Trust, and Integrity on the real issues facing you today, and address these questions, there will be another 100 questions confronting you when you meet next. It may then be too late to reverse the negative route you have taken. Further procrastination will only result in your running out of time…

4. **What happened finally…Conclusions:**

4.1. The Group Chairman maintained that he has done his best for everyone but yet nobody is happy. In our very first meeting, there was 100% agreement from everyone present that they were not satisfied or happy.

4.2. All the subsequent meetings have not changed the above situation: Nobody is happy.

4.3. I have given much thought to this issue, and I have noted that none of the FMBs really care for Growth,

Diversification, Results, Modernization, Management Upgrading, etc.

4.4. The focus and interest of all the FMBs are on extracting more money and property from the Chairman.

4.5. The Chairman, in turn, has total control of the above, and he is aware that his continued value to the other Group members and power over them, can be sustained indefinitely only so long as he fully controls Group/Family Accounting, Money, and Property.

4.6. It is also true that the FMBs have, till now, been grateful to the Chairman for having inducted them into business and wealth through his pioneering efforts over the last 40 years.

4.7. Unfortunately, the Chairman has not realized that all the FMBs and their respective families are now only focused on what the Chairman can do for them in the future – the gratefulness for the past has now dissipated and is no longer relevant.

4.8. Obviously, what the Chairman could accomplish in his younger days is totally different from what he can do now as a much older person. Therefore, the Chairman has set up a 'system' of his own which is based on disbursing favours and controlling all monetary resources.

4.9. As of today, more than half of the able-bodied men in the Group are under-employed, but all of them are paid salaries and enjoy perks like housing, cars, etc. The Group has not provided them with hard-working opportunities to justify their earnings, and at the same time, they do not have the guts to exit and become independently successful. The irony is that even such people are unhappy!

4.10. The very few people who have had an opportunity have made themselves indispensable but are unhappy because they just cannot get to do what they want…all resources are controlled by the Chairman.

4.11. The Chairman, in such a situation, sees himself as secure and, other than superficial desire to do something to make people happy, he is not doing anything in particular.

4.12. What the Chairman does not see, or appreciate, is the fact that he has carefully nurtured a Family Business culture that will most definitely fall apart once his influence is over, in terms of his control on resources.

4.13. The whole structure of the Family Business is extremely weak both in terms of Group Management Structure and Control and in terms of the total absence of Values that keep families together in a family business.

4.14. Every meeting makes it obvious that nobody really cares for the long-term well-being of the business or of the Group. There is utter selfishness on all sides, a total absence of trust, and no loyalty to any entity that can hold the families together.

4.15. Overall, as of now, the situation is a hopeless one…unless, of course, the Chairman realizes immediately that emotional outbursts and emotional blackmail, and monopolizing power over resources, and without transparent accounting, and doling out favours, only builds superficial loyalty and promotes loss of integrity and trust within the family business, and within the families.

4.16. There is hope if the Chairman wakes up before it is too late. Once he understands his legitimate duties to the Family Business (and consequently to families), he can demand the same from the others. There is still time for him to become a Great Leader – and there is an urgent need for a Great Leader to save the Punjewal Group.

5. **The End:**

Three years after I had withdrawn from my association with the Punjewal Group, I got calls both from the Chairman and from one of his brothers requesting me to visit them as their Family Business situation had deteriorated. While I was appreciative of the fact that they had finally seen sense in my advice to them, and they now obviously regretted their inaction, it was just too late to get back lost ground. My final letter to the Chairman:

"A couple of months ago, you had called me suggesting a visit as my assistance was urgently required. Immediately after, your brother had also called for the same purpose. I appreciate that I am remembered perhaps for some of my advice given earlier. After some critical investigation, following up on your calls, I am constrained to advise you as follows:

1. During the time of my interaction with all of you, the differences within the family were all concerned with the sharing of money and wealth, and the process was fueled by extreme mutual distrust. The successful running of the Family Business and of mapping its future was a low priority confounded with questionable ethics in running the Family Business.

2. My main role as a Consultant to Family Businesses is to ensure their success and growth across future generations. I believe that a family will be happy, united, and prosperous only if the Family Business is managed successfully and grows continuously building a brand and a great reputation that will take it into the Future. I was obviously unsuccessful in converting your thinking to this direction.

3. I, therefore, recommend that the only practical solution at this late stage is to approach a reputed Arbitration Firm that will help the whole family divide all assets and liabilities fairly and peacefully. If even this process is delayed further, then I can only advise that the net asset value to be divided will decrease further with the obvious increase in liabilities.

4. The above is serious advice and I do hope you will all explore this without delay, if not already attempted.

Once again, thank you for having thought of me.
With best wishes, and regards,

Raju"

40

Client Experience: PluDor Manufacturing Ltd.: First and Second Generation Family Business in stagnation, and in serious conflict, but unanimously desiring a solution to stay together

1. **Background:**

    1.1. A 50-year-old multi-family family business managed by the Founder Generation and the second generation.

    1.2. Multi-location, Multi-product Speciality Sector Manufacturing with significant export business.

    1.3. A world leader in a particular product in a particular segment.

    1.4. Prominent in business circles is the state of their origin where plants are in multiple locations.

    1.5. Listed on BSE/NSE.

2. **Issues:**

    2.1. It is a complex family business comprising four independent families from one Branch, and a fifth family unrelated to the other four.

    2.2. They have been in business together for 50 years.

    2.3. Five elders including the three founders/five business active second-generation members.

2.4. By mutual agreement, every Elder Generation Member is entitled to induct only ONE of his children into the family business. This has been a major plus-point in exploring solutions to major family business issues.

2.5. All well-educated, with engineering degrees. The second-generation members are also MBAs.

2.6. **Amid business stagnation, there was an absence of focused leadership, lack of clarity on decision making and accountability, absence of organized, agenda-based communication, and pressures of nepotism in a loose management structure.**

2.7. **They had reached a point of having to decide whether to stick together or to part ways.**

2.8. My entry, through a third-party reference and an introductory meeting and presentation on my work with other clients, was a last-ditch effort at finding a solution to stay together.

3. **Progress: Our association is now in its fifth year, and currently, as I write, in an advanced phase of positive transformation.**

4. **Transformation: Phase 1: Structured Action-Motivating Communication:**

    4.1. Started with individual (1-on-1) meetings approximating 1.5 hours each.

    4.2. Was able to establish that irrespective of uncertainty and tensions, the desire to stay together was there but without knowing how. This 'desire' was a positive discovery for me to work on.

4.3. Differences were over power-sharing, nepotism, conflict of interest, and accountability but not about money, wealth, or property. This was a blessing and a positive reinforcement to my effort.

4.4. Set up the 'Family Council' with all the FMBs as members.

4.5. The Family Council Chairman is one of the founders and was a unanimous choice, unrelated to hierarchy and politics. At the same time, his choice was strategically appropriate for the transformation exercise.

4.6. Meeting at least once a month for the last FOUR years plus, with formal agenda, open discussion, follow-through notes, and continuous follow-up on action taken. With COVID-19 restrictions, the Family Council Meetings have switched to online mode.

4.7. The formation and effective functioning of the Family Council has resulted in better mutual understanding and a strong desire to improve the overall management of the PluDor Group.

5. **Transformation: Phase 2: Accepting the new principles of change:**

    5.1. Accepting the need for a well-defined, result-oriented, accountable Management and Organization Structure to remove weaknesses of overlapping designations and management roles that confused employees and weakened the Performance Delivery System.

    5.2. Successfully launched the process of Accountable Management through Business Planning, Budgeting, and Target-driven management processes in every company and division, with high-pressure motivation to deliver as per forecast and targets.

5.3. The pressure to deliver targeted performance began with the Family Managers to start with.

5.4. Acceptance of the logic that the families behind a family business can be happy and united only if the family business is continuously performing well while also enhancing investor wealth as well as reputation in society.

6. **Transformation: Phase 3: Implementation of Change: Growth Plans, Performance Upgrading, Operational Succession:**

    6.1. Therefore, accepted and started implementing the strategy of 'Growth as the Key to Family Business Success'.

    6.2. Now, Business Planning, Budgeting, and Target-setting exercise include a minimum of three years' Forward Planning to prepare well in advance to meet growth objectives. The actual performance of the PluDor companies and divisions has improved with an active emphasis on accountability for achieving growth-oriented performance and results.

    6.3. The above improvements have also been made possible by the senior generation delegating all Operational Management Responsibility to the younger generation and bringing about a more 'professional interface' both within members of the Family Council and between the younger generation and the key professional managers and employees of the Group Companies and Divisions.

    6.4. The management style of the younger generation is now increasingly professional and performance-driven and is positively influencing a change in the work culture across all Companies and Divisions.

6.5. The Family Council is constantly and consistently supervising, motivating, and strengthening the transformation process across all aspects of successfully managing the family business.

6.6. The bonds within the multi-generational members of the Family Council have only become stronger through this profoundly serious effort within the Family Council.

7. **Transformation: Phase 4: Family Constitution:**

   7.1. A stage was reached where the multi-generational members of the Family Council, belonging to multiple families, understood the advantages of associating together productively, over a long and foreseeable period, and therefore decided to formulate a Family Constitution.

   7.2. The Family Constitution will mutually bind them, to follow certain minimum rules of engagement, in mutually connected areas of business activity, resulting in a profitable partnership with peace and harmony, over a period of time.

   7.3. The success of a family business is often judged by its capacity to survive over many generations, and I expect the PluDor Group FMBs will do their best to meet this precious objective. A Family Constitution makes sense only when there is a strong desire to stay together over generations.

8. **Transformation: Phase 5: 'Letting Go' towards Management Succession:**

   8.1. 'Letting Go' has become a somewhat serious problem particularly in recent years as older generations are fitter in their late sixties and seventies, even while younger generations aspire for greater responsibilities in their thirties and forties.

8.2. In many cases, 'Letting Go' to ease succession can be facilitated by an attractive and productive Retirement Policy where the 'Elder' will continue to enjoy certain perks of higher management, but without direct and actual operational or strategic responsibility, that will support one's social and economic status in business circles and community.

8.3. 'Letting Go' may not always be a pleasant exercise, depending on inter-family relationships, organizational health, and the insecurities of the elder generation,

8.4. However, in PluDor, since the potential 'Successors' are sons of the founding generation, and since the progress, performance, and prospects of the company and its divisions have seen positive growth since operations were handed over to the younger generation, the issue of 'Letting Go' was approached to create a win-win solution for all sides.

8.5. Broadly, the five members of the founder generation were willing to hand over management succession to the younger generation with the following steps agreed upon:

8.5.1. The Elders would continue to occupy Non-Executive Board positions as per statutory and legal permissions and entitlements up to the permitted maximum age.

8.5.2. The Elders would continue to be active members of the Family Council up to the age of 75 but extendable up to 80 years, health permitting, and subject to conditions specified in the Family Constitution.

8.5.3. As active members of the Family Council, and given their contribution and experience, Elders will assist the younger generation, when requested and assist in promoting and strengthening the professionalization of the PluDor Group Companies and Divisions.

8.5.4. Elders will continue to play an active leadership role of key industry associations and institutions of national importance to further promote the reputation of PluDor Group Companies as well as of the related industry to which PluDor is associated.

8.5.5. Elders will continue to lead CSR activities on behalf of the PluDor Group Companies and Divisions.

8.5.6. The Elders' Retirement Policy will be as agreed to in the Family Constitution and will protect their respective last earned official income and benefits.

9. **Transformation: Phase 6: The Mission for the Future: Professionalization: Upgrading management and work culture:**

   1. Continuously Planning/Setting/Executing/Meeting Performance Targets: Top line and bottom line.

   2. Telescoping/overlapping Growth Plans on a minimum three-yearly basis.

3. Performance priorities include attaining and maintaining a high level of industry competitiveness and industry leadership.

4. Achieving shareholder and market acceptance of growth and performance leading to continuous appreciation in market capitalization.

5. Key managers accountable for clear performance targets in their respective/functional areas/departments.

6. Zero Defect Manufacturing and Work Processes.

7. Zero Waste Manufacturing and Work Processes.

8. Timely and effective compliance to Legal and Statutory Obligations that wins the respect of Government Depatments/Officers.

9. HR plus HRD to ensure Training, Career Development, Promotional Avenues for retention of Key Employees.

10. Clean, Green, Safe, Hygienic, Disciplined Employee Friendly but Performance Demanding Work Environment.

11. Clean, Green, Healthy, Nature-friendly Aesthetically Designed External Landscaped Environment.

12. Customer Friendly, Visitor Friendly Entry Gate Security and Office Reception.

13. Other emerging areas of advancement to be continuously observed and studied for application in PluDor Group Companies.

14. Global Expansion.

41

Client Experience: Work in Process: CB Group: Charanjibhai Brothers & Co. Ltd (Est. 1905): Objective: Peaceful separation, succession...so the next and future generations may live their lives independently and in harmony

1. **Family Business Background:**

    1.1. Third Generation Management through three male cousins.

    1.2. Eldest cousin, Naveenbhai, 76, professionally qualified from a prominent American University, is the Chairman of the Group Holding Company, and favours a dictatorial management style, with no hint of retirement.

    1.3. Cousin 2, Pawanbhai and Cousin 3, Vikrambhai, are in their early sixties.

    1.4. Naveenbhai independently controls and manages the 100 Years' old Processed Herbal Root Product (PHRP) Division where all the cousins have an equal shareholding. He is assisted by his daughter, Rupali – a clear case of nepotism. Pawanbhai had run the PHRP Business in the past and was always seen as a supporter of Naveenbhai.

1.5. Rupali independently manages the relatively new Biscuits Division fully financed and supported by the PHRP Division.

1.6. Naveenbhai and Vikrambhai visibly dislike each other and have many disagreements.

1.7. Pawanbhai lives in a different location and manages a New Business Division (NBD) independently and prefers peaceful coexistence until the retirement of Naveenbhai. All the cousins are shareholders in this New Business Division.

1.8. Vikrambhai independently manages a potentially promising branded FMCG Product Division along with his daughters. All the cousins are shareholders in this FMCG Division.

1.9. All have only daughters in their families, but the daughters are well educated and have full freedom to actively participate in the Family Business.

1.10. Disagreements relate to exercising management decision-making power and not about money and wealth. Inter-personal and inter-family trust and integrity are exceptionally high on financial matters.

1.11. The traditional 100 years old PHRP business is very profitable, but the market is shrinking due to changing consumption norms influenced by Government legislation and laws. It is a matter of time before this business will inevitably close.

2. **My assessment of the family business and relationships** after observing dialogues and debates at the Family Council Meetings over six months:

2.1. Relationships hang delicately by a thin thread, weighed down by tensions and uncertainty, only barely held together by the still profitable, original, traditionally processed herbal roots business – PHRP – staying afloat in a shrinking market.

2.2. Age and medical fitness of the three cousins are against taking a long-term view about the future of the togetherness of the three families.

2.3. Productive Management Succession towards an optimistic future for the PHRP Division is a question mark.

2.4. The two diversified businesses of NBRD and Biscuits are yet to take off in terms of expected performance projections, although the FMCG subsidiary is on a sound development track with good brand acceptance and excellent market potential.

2.5. The strained family relationships within or outside the Family Council are such that neither corrective business action nor accountability for delivering business performance, are enforceable in any of the businesses.

2.6. Being blind to the tensions as above and prolonging the agony will worsen the situation through avoidance and delays.

2.7. I am clear that given the circumstances, there is nothing wrong, by reputation or conduct or deed, for leaders of Promoter Families at a particular stage of the Family Business, to realistically assess their situation and decide to embark on the inevitable mission to accomplish a win-win settlement that leads to a 'mutually beneficial, legal, fair, equitable, graceful, and peaceful separation of business interests'.

2.8. I do not doubt that each family's future generations will be appreciative of the understanding with which the 'mission' was accomplished. They would have been saved from the mess that multiplying uncertainties bring in the form of confusion and chaos and antagonism that otherwise would have been bequeathed to them by a neglectful older generation.

3. **My Recommended Solutions: PHRP Division: Phase out and close in three years or less…**

3.1. I do not agree with the view that the Processed Herbal Roots Division should be allowed to run its course until it dies a natural death.

3.2. While I may agree that right now the Roots Division is not a sinking ship, but, at the same time, I believe that this 'ship of hope' is sailing in a rapidly shrinking ocean. If the ship can float indefinitely on speculative hope, then without doubt the serious possibility exists that **without warning the ship can self-destruct** as it hits rocks at the bottom of the ocean when the water disappears.

3.3. To ensure definite value to all stakeholders, the 'ship' must be saved intact while it is still afloat.

3.4. All stakeholders, including employees of all categories, can be taken care of without guilt with realistic planning. Speculative greed to extract something till the very end can also destroy value through unforeseen happenings, much like the stock market.

3.5. 'Profitable exit in time' must be the strategy. To me, considering the family circumstances explained above, three years is realistic keeping in mind the age and medical fitness of the key family heads.

4. **My Recommended Solutions: Biscuits Division: Uncertain Future: Merge with FMCG Business…**

   4.1. Going by what was stated at the Family Council Meeting, PHRP with a shrinking market but financial strength cannot stand on its own without Biscuits and the still-to-establish Biscuits Division cannot survive without PHRP.

   4.2. Biscuits today is more expense than revenue, with no profit.

   4.3. In its current state, it has no future.

   4.4. Future nurturing of this product line as a stand-alone is also doubtful as Naveenbhai has made it clear that Rupali's priority is her own family first and attention to the Biscuits business will be only in the time she can spare beyond her own family time.

   4.5. Since some investments have been made, a merger with the FMCG Product Division may be a solution.

5. **Recommended Solution: FMCG Product Division: Hive off to become an independent 'Vikrambhai Family Business'**

   5.1. Irrespective of Vikrambhai's uncertain responses during the discussion on hiving off of the FMCG Division from the Family Holding Company, I must confess that he is a lucky person for having been given the opportunity to manage the FMCG business. It is an exceptionally good FMCG brand with high growth and market potential, compared to the declining PHDP Business and the relatively untried NBD in its current state.

5.2. If the FMCG Division is not performing as it should or is not producing the desired results, that is a management problem and not attributable to competition or other FMCG variables that are a given in such a 'me-too' sector.

5.3. With the type of resources that have been at his command, and without the pressure of accountability to perform to growth targets, he has had a lot of freedom to do just about anything he wants.

5.4. Honestly, the hiving off is a great opportunity for Vikrambhai to have back-to-back strategies to design the FMCG Division into a leading and profitable FMCG company in its product field in India. Back-to-back strategies could include getting in a very capable co-investor partner with the desired expertise, resources, and energy to move radically forward and make up for the slippages of the past. There could also be other beneficial options.

5.5. Vikrambhai may have problems with various issues with his cousins, but FMCG Division cannot be one of them. He has been lucky and it is up to him to convert luck into opportunity.

6. **Recommended Solution: New Business Division: To be transferred totally to 'Pawanbhai Family' simultaneous to the closure of PHRP Business or earlier.**

   6.1. Right now, the future of the NBD is uncertain, for many reasons, and in course of addressing the actions recommended, an appropriate decision in everybody's interest needs to be taken.

6.2. In the interim, Pawanbhai is under-employed and Naveenbhai inducting him into the PHRP Division at this critical time will be a great support to move forward on the recommended strategy.

6.3. Fortunately, while Naveenbhai and Pawanbhai may not agree on certain matters, both are familiar with the intricacies of the PHRP Business and with the executives/employees who are part of it. And Pawanbhai has worked in the PHRP Division before.

6.4. Therefore, I expect them to work together with the right balance of power, energy, experience, strategy, and common sense to exit from the PHRP Business peacefully and profitably in three years.

6.5. The challenge of such radical change cannot be under-estimated: Naveenbhai's maturity and experience and Pawanbhai's energy and sense of mission must come together to benefit all concerned, particularly the next and future generations.

7. **Recommended Solution: Other Divisible Assets and Investments:** These can be listed, and the right decisions can be taken as per mutual agreement.

   7.1. **Indivisible Complex Assets:** My first thought is the formation of an appropriate Multi-Family Trust that can administer such assets and ensure the flow of benefits arising therefrom to all the interested families and individuals. Maybe the new Family Holding Company can be converted to a Multiple Family Trust.

7.2. **Charitable Activities and Community Services:** *It would be good if the families can continue to be together on these activities and create a Trust and a Forum that can be the meeting ground for perpetuating the links from the past. It can never be forgotten that irrespective of the state of relationships today, the current and past generations have been responsible for the accumulation of wealth for all the families.*

7.3. It is my strong recommendation that since a professional firm of repute will be commissioned to handle the hiving off of the FMCG Division, activity on other fronts should be taken up without delay again using the same or similar professional services.

7.4. The Family Council will also have to agree on a common strategy across the Divisions and locations on how the planned activity is going to be represented to prevent loose talk and feeling of insecurity among key employees. *At the same time, it must be understood that prolonging an uncertain situation with declining relationships in a stagnant business situation with ageing partners will provoke employees into indiscipline and politics which can only do more harm all around.*

8. It is of course possible that I may have overlooked certain issues or facts not within my understanding but of which the Family Council Members are aware, and such issues and facts need to be considered in the decision-making process.

9. My request to Naveenbhai is that at this critical time, to ensure a successful outcome of this important 'Mission' to all concerned, and again in the interest of the next and future generations, he should be less of a cousin and more of

a Patriarch, both as the most senior Elder and as the Chairman of the Family Council.

10. Finally, despite personal and professional differences, because there is mutual financial trust and integrity, Succession is not likely to be an issue as and when the above processes are complete.

42

Client Experience: Mehsangir Engineering: Conflict breeding suspicion: My mail to a client expressing surprise and disappointment over an incident affecting the progress of our joint effort.

1. After all the effort and time we have devoted to the 'Unity through Growth' effort, the deliberations yesterday, once again went downhill even to the extent of dragging my reputation in the mud through loose and personally insulting remarks.

2. Please understand that I represent each one of you in this Mission and I must be fair in this task by highlighting all views before a decision can be taken. It is unfortunate that the degree of mutual distrust among you is still so high, not only below the surface but also visible to all, even to the extent of suspecting my motivations????

3. It is now abundantly clear to me that all of you can work together as a Single United Family in the Family Business ONLY, repeat ONLY, if results of all Divisions are consistently high and, simultaneously, with clarity on the planned and implementable future of the two main Divisions. Unfortunately, the picture on these fronts continues to be unclear, and there is little or no documentation of effort so far to establish trust or accountability or capability in the commitment to these objectives.

4. In these circumstances, where the two key Divisions Myflo and Mortel exhibit serious negatives, the Myflo Product Division tends to be viewed as a 'Superman'. Imagine what will happen if Superman Myflo is confronted by an unexpected market or competitive or organizational situation... Do you all sincerely think that you can survive as the United Mehsangir Family since a blame-game will automatically take over with declining performance and growth?

5. The lesson you still need to learn is that you will all be 'family' only if results are good and growth happens, continuously. Without positive results and growth, the Mehsangir Family is '0'.

6. Therefore, the Family Council Meeting next month is most critical to decide whether it is worthwhile for all of you to continue the 'Unity through Growth' effort or find a decent way to bury it.

7. Please understand that it will be an unproductive and useless exercise to try and assign blame to any one person or family for the breakdown: *"Hamam may sub nange hote hain"* is a wise old saying based on the study of the history of human behaviour over many generations.

8. It is now up to all of you to save 'Unity through Growth'... The situation is not to be taken lightly.

9. I suggest that you – the Mehsangir Family – revisit your decision to continue with my assistance based on the outcome of next month's Family Council Meeting and Budget/Business Plan Presentations for the coming year.

10. The Quality, Commitment, Accountability and Truth behind these presentations will help you decide where you want to

go. I am, of course, with you only with your trust, and if you think I will be genuinely useful.

The family was clear that they wanted me to continue. Attitudes and progress turned positive with increased mutual trust.

43

Client Experience: Petran Process Materials Ltd.: Good Families, Good People, Short-sighted by 'Power Shortage', Fight…Winner at great expense, Loser has nothing to show…

1. In one of the family businesses, I was involved in, a listed company, the Founder, on his death, had left behind two sons and a nephew, of a similar age group, and all well qualified, but only two businesses. Eventually, intense rivalry to head the larger company by a son and the nephew resulted in serious family conflict leading finally to a very expensive and dirty battle to buy and corner shares in the stock market. It took the winning family many, many years to recover from the heavy financial damage, with some permanent adverse consequences. If only the Founder had left **three** businesses, there would have been no problem.

2. **Some reasons:**

    2.1. One of the major weaknesses of the family in business was the apparent absence of visionary thinking and preparing for the future.

    2.2. Every action seems to be aimed at the here-and-now, with a defence that the future of the business is not predictable, because of the nature of the business itself.

2.3. And then, of course, like in many families in business, no one in the family likes to be held accountable.

2.4. Lack of concern for the future resulted in more people chasing lesser opportunities. In such a situation, conflict and stresses and strains are inevitable, and even more so when wealth creation is hampered by a lack of choices for compensating for the ups and downs.

2.5. Finally, due to the absence of forward thinking, the next generation of capable youngsters who can be inducted into the business, plus the next generation of investors will be left holding the baggage of the past as the legacy for the future.

2.6. A negative legacy with limited choices is a dangerous mixture, offering no scope for positive adjustments.

2.7. I don't have all the answers, but I do know that the responsibility for leading a productive, healthy, and peaceful 'senior citizen' life, and for providing a better future, to the next generation, of your own families, particularly in terms of preparation, and in terms of financial and mental well-being, lies squarely with the four Seniors in the family business.

And the serious problem in this statement is the fact that if 50% of the seniors are in a long-drawn conflict, the other 50% will be rendered ineffective, and therefore a negative legacy is a foregone conclusion.

44

Family Business: Tensions and disharmony rise proportionately with rise in uncertainty and stagnation.

(This is a true story, and it struck me that if a Family Business with multiple families and family members, was to become a victim of business stagnation and uncertainty about its recovery, their experience would be similar to that of the people caught in a stranded elevator... suspicion, conflict, and worse, would take a similar turn, and, when recovery happens, relationships will never return to what they used to be in better times.)

There were eight people in the elevator of a prominent office building in a well-known city. They worked for different organizations but were familiar with each other because the routine of morning entry and evening exit was almost the same, every day.

On a normal end-of-a-busy-day evening, between Floors 13 and 14, the elevator stalled. It was 5.43 PM, and, the Elevator Group, what we will now identify them as, was a reasonably happy lot. They were looking forward to an evening of de-stressing before another stressful workday tomorrow.

By 5.45, the elevator had yet not moved. The alarm switch was pressed. The Elevator Group now spontaneously reacted with mutual hope and encouragement: "These things happen, you know. I was stuck like this last year and we came out alright... turned out to be a minor short circuit... etc."

It was now 5.48. There had been no response to the pressing of the alarm button. Their mobiles did not work in the elevator. No reassuring noises could be heard from the outside. Fortunately, the elevator light was on. There was still an atmosphere of hope, but the group was getting fidgety.

At 5.51, the first signs of enquiring restlessness: "Wonder what's wrong… never happened for this long before…"

At 5.52, a 'leader' of the Elevator Group emerged from among the eight. Cheerful, bubbling, comforting, experienced, knowledgeable, definite…. made everybody feel that the situation was normal in such a circumstance. Yes, a little discomfort, but not to worry. Motivated some small chat, smiles, and even laughter.

At 5.58, the elevator had still not moved. The 'leader' was looked up to expectantly for an answer. He had none. In fact, he was irritated at people expecting him to know everything!

There were no other claims to 'leadership'.

By 6.01, the Elevator Group was leaderless, answerless and without hope: Is this elevator ever going to move? When??

At 6.06, they were beginning to feel hot and sweaty. Discomfort and worry could no longer be hidden. Why was nothing happening??

At 6.10, one of the Elevator Group Members, as if revealing a triumphant discovery, announced that the elevator's capacity was seven, NOT eight! And because there was an eighth person on board, the elevator was stuck and giving the rest a bad time. It was as if they were struck by a revelation. Yes, that must be it. But who among them was No.8?

By 6.14, there was no Elevator Group. Instead, there were eight suspicious, unhappy, angry individuals. Who was the culprit? And why could he, or she, not have waited for the next trip??

At 6.18, somebody threw up the suggestion that the elevator stoppage was deliberate sabotage.

At 6.19, the elevator moved. There was dead silence – and mutual avoidance of eye contact. The small sign which was now visible when one of them moved towards the front said: 'Elevator Capacity: 10'.

In 36 minutes of uncertainty, eight normal people let their imagination run wild and developed mistrust towards each other.

45

A Family Office for Family Welfare

It is advisable for a Family Business – multi-family or otherwise – to set up a Family Office to take care of the funding of expenses that cannot legitimately be expensed to the Family Business Entity. The funding of the Family Office will be through the Family Business Beneficiaries in terms of those family members directly involved in the management of the family business. The funds so generated will become the 'wealth' that will grow perpetually through growth-based investments.

Broadly, the Family Office will take care of:

1. Retirement Income/Pension for Family Members retiring from the Family Business.
2. Higher education needs of the children of partner families.
3. Professional development of impending entrants to the family business as part of their entry preparation.
4. Insurance needs of all partner families.
5. Funding for family emergencies, celebrations, get-togethers.
6. Family welfare with regard to taking care of partner family members and their families who may not qualify professionally for entry into the management of the family business. This is important to prevent feelings of injustice that can aggravate into family issues and conflicts that can affect the profitable functioning of the Family Business.

7. Family Charities distinct from CSR linked to the Family Business.

8. Contributions to other avenues mutually agreed upon.

A Model OrgChart for Family Business

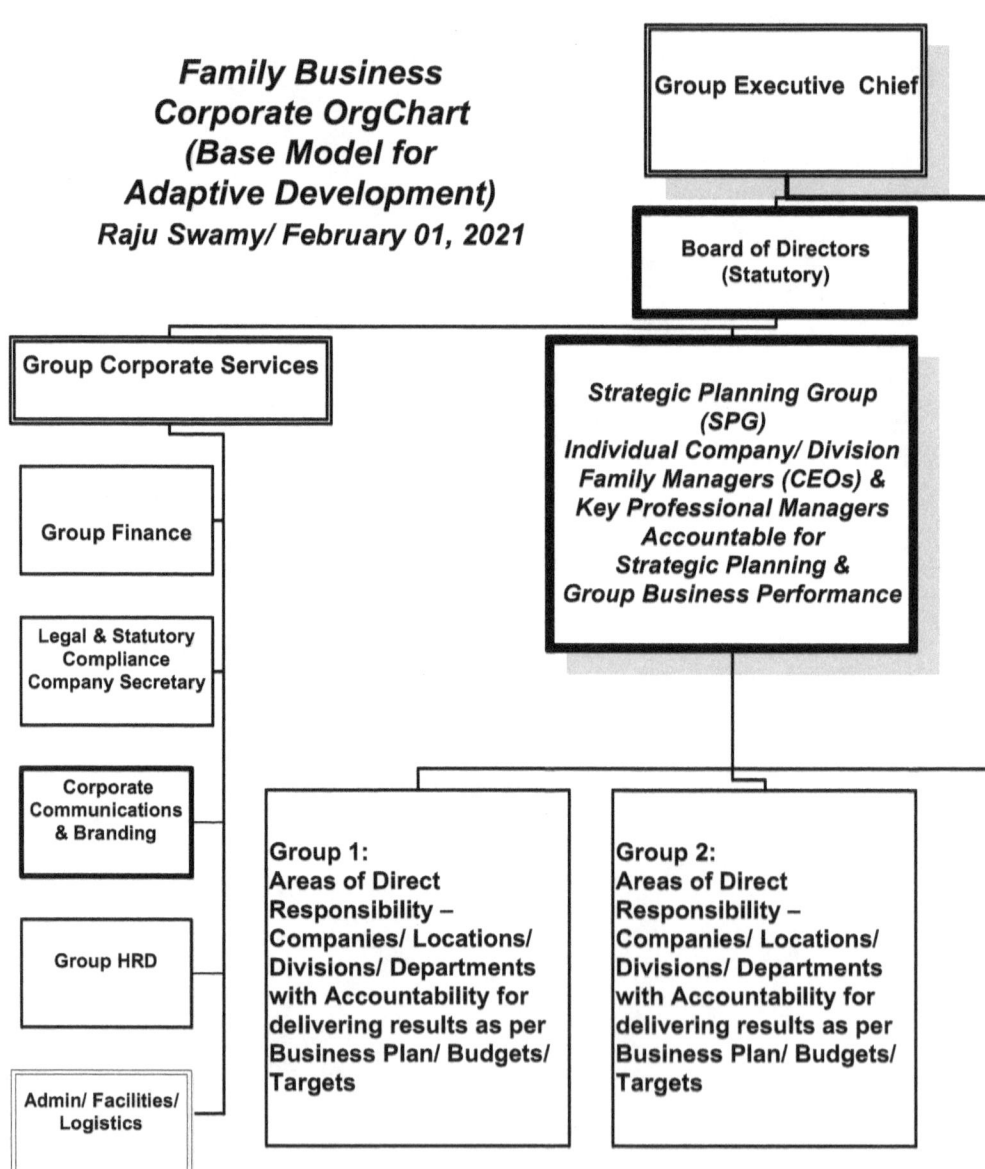

```
┌─────────────────────────────┐
│      Family Council         │
│ (All Family Members directly│
│  involved in management of  │
│    the Family Business)     │
└─────────────────────────────┘
             │
             ├──────────────────────────┐
             │              ┌───────────────────────┐
             │              │    Family Office      │
             │              └───────────────────────┘
             │                          │
             │              ┌───────────────────────┐
             │              │   Funding Pipeline    │
             │              │    to Family Office   │
             │              └───────────────────────┘
             │                          │
             │              ┌───────────────────────┐
             │              │  Investment & Wealth  │
             │              │      Management       │
             │              └───────────────────────┘
             │                          │
             │              ┌───────────────────────┐
             │              │   Retirement Funding  │
             │              └───────────────────────┘
             │                          │
┌────────────────────────┐  ┌───────────────────────┐
│ Group 3:               │  │  Family Trust Fund    │
│ Areas of Direct        │  │ Welfare/ Celebrations/│
│ Responsibility –       │  │ Emergencies/ Insurance│
│ Companies/ Locations/  │  └───────────────────────┘
│ Divisions/ Departments │              │
│ with Accountability for│  ┌───────────────────────┐
│ delivering results as  │  │     Professional      │
│ per Business Plan/     │  │     Development       │
│ Budgets/ Targets       │  └───────────────────────┘
└────────────────────────┘              │
                            ┌───────────────────────┐
                            │    Foundation for     │
                            │   Community Social    │
                            │     Development       │
                            └───────────────────────┘
```

47

A Moment of Truth... SWOT Analysis of a 105-year-old Family Business currently managed by the 4th Generation....

*F*acing a moment of truth today can fuel the future with new aspirations and competitive energy – and consequent ongoing positives for the present and future generations of the Trivistral Group Families.

SWOT Analysis

Strengths:

1. Foundation of strong Inherited Personal/Family Financial Security
2. Internal Integrity
3. Absence of Conflict
4. Conservative, Non-ostentatious, Paternal Business Outlook
5. 'Running' businesses with opportunity and leverage to grow
6. Resources to support change
7. Age potential of the younger generation

Weaknesses:

1. Absence of Greed is Strength, but, Absence of Aspiration is a Weakness.

2. Vision – Where do we want to go – for what – when – why.

3. Education/Training…inadequate for the 4th Generation by current standards. While the next generation must get the best education in the world, to be able to manage a business, the current generation must make it up through world-class entrepreneurial programs, to be competitive strategic thinkers, and also to be able to hire and manage highly qualified professionals.

4. Competitive Entrepreneurial Energy and Motivation.

5. Dependence on 'fait accompli' and acceptance of status quo…. lack of result-orientation

6. Work as a ritual and not as a mission to achieve. No goals… little initiative….

7. Approach to Business as a 'benevolent, secure landlord with a 9-to-5 job.'

8. Very old-fashioned paternalistic concern for people.

9. A total absence of strategic thinking.

10. Away from the business mainstream network, in India and abroad.

11. S l o w…disinterested…lost.

12. Absence of a 'cash cow'.

13. Lack of interest/concern for brand building.

14. Marketing.

15. Excessive dependence on single sector distribution.

16. Accountability.

Opportunities:
1. **Infinite… with your resources**
2. **You must look for them – they won't come to you**
3. **You have to look at the world as your market**
4. **Create time for 'opportunity', not for work – there will be people who will work for you**

Threats:
1. Falling business growth erodes both wealth and confidence.
2. Stagnation breeds conflict breeds distrust.
3. Conflict tends to multiply rapidly, with and without reason.
4. Negative emotions overtake reason, prevent damage control. Everyone loses, now and into the future.
5. **Time runs out, on you, when action is scarce, and you do not know where you are going….**

Wake up, for the world is yours if you want it. Your forefathers gave you a head start, and you have no excuse to falter. And, *you have nothing to lose when you do well.*

A Gentle Reminder… you are in charge, your job description is clear, and it is always larger than what you may have assumed. You can never not have time. You can never not have things to discuss. You can never not have time to lead. You can never not have time to succeed. Bring about a productive way of facing the challenge of the present and future. Inspire the next generation – perpetuate a larger Family Business riding on to the next century… there are no excuses!

Ask yourself this fundamental question:

Should inheritance boost the capacity to achieve,
or
should inheritance give you the right to be complacent?
Who wins in the end?

48

Profit

1. 'Profit' is not a bad word. It is your reward for delivering what a customer wants at a price he or she is willing to pay—obviously more than the cost you have incurred in making it available.

2. Profit is your incentive to get into business. Being able to make a profit through legitimate means reflects positively on your values, on your enterprise, originality, initiative, creativity, competitiveness, and your skills in multiplying your ability to invest, and to grow your business.

3. And in the process of ideation, visualizing, and executing your Business Enterprise, you are creating employment, direct and indirect, and meeting the needs of society.

4. And all this while, your benefits also flow into your family and you are laying the foundation for a Family Business, seeded with your brainpower, values, and your dreams, and you no longer have limitations on how far you can go.

5. There are good people who will say "Money is not everything". True, but it is difficult to donate to charity, or to run schools, or to help people in distress unless you continuously earn money, create wealth, and use that wealth both as capital to grow your business and to grow your income from which you contribute to the service of the deserving.

6. Yes, if you earn but do not contribute, you will become fat, unhealthy, sick, frustrated, useless, and slide even as a Family Business, without 'Values'.

7. A Family Business driven by 'Values' is the ultimate contributor to society and an asset to the nation.

49

So, finally, if you think you need assistance, and if I were to advise and escort you towards desirable change, what would the 'Take-Off" preparation look like? This is exactly the process I have followed with most clients...

1. *Let us agree on 'Why' you need assistance:*

    1.1. At some point in a Family's existence, family members begin to question themselves on whether they, as individuals and as constituent families, are meeting their goals and aspirations. **Is the Family Business delivering according to expectations, helping them to fulfill personal and family desires on values, growth, wealth, and security, and therefore of peace within the Family? How will social status and financial security be ensured when active family professionals reach a stage of retirement?**

    1.2. In this context, it is imperative to understand that when families are together in business, business ups and downs can influence even emotional bonds of the Family, if not resolved in time. Primarily, Family Wealth grows from the Family Business. Good Business Performance is good for the Family. Bad Business Performance is bad for the Family. Simple logic. We need Good Business Performance to support and promote Family Values, Wealth, and Well-being. *It is pleasant to share profits but unpleasant to share losses, particularly where the light at the end of the tunnel depends only on hope rather than on being supported by facts and figures.*

1.3. Therefore, we need to make a clear distinction between understanding within the Family and understanding within the Family Business Group. The Family Business Group fuels the well-being of the Family. Mixing Family issues with Business issues constantly over a long period creates problems at both ends as real issues never get resolved because of mutual avoidance of reality out of fear of the consequences. Solutions must necessarily address both the well-being of constituent families and of the Family Business in terms of structure, policies, processes, and standards that will ensure Business Performance. **It must be understood without ambiguity that Family Well-being is dependent on sustained success of the Family Business. A predominantly merit-based Family Business will ensure Family Well-being in the long run even during bad times. That is the strength of a Good Family Business.**

1.4. In the language of Family Business Governance, is it possible for the Family Business to separate 'Ownership' from 'Management', so that the 'Family' maximizes its returns from the Family Business?

2. *Once we have agreed, comprehensively and unambiguously, on the 'Why', 'How' will I approach my 'Mission':* I cannot provide the entire strategy till I get to know all of you individually and as Individual Business Teams and as a Group, but broadly this will be the 'Take-Off' road map in terms of the first phase of Action Points:

2.1. Introductory Presentation and discussion with all the members of the Family Business – whoever you want to include - to reach a consensus on 'Issues to be addressed' and 'Goals to be achieved', within a mutually acceptable time frame.

2.2. As we progress, non- working/non-managing family members will not be included in the deliberations. Only FMBs (Family Members in Business) will be included. These are Family Members who necessarily have active management and operational roles in the Family Business.

2.3. Identification of a Logistics Coordinator, and of the FMB Group (this will at some point convert to the Family Council with all FMBs included), that will assist the Advisor on behalf of the Family to successfully carry through the assignment.

2.4. 'One-on-One' Meetings with each member of the FMB Group to understand individual aspirations, and of personal suggestions on total improvement of the Family Business, to meet Business, Family, and Individual aspirations. The 'One-on-One' Meetings will on an average require about 1.5 to 2 hours per meeting per person without diversions of any kind.

2.5. Individual Meetings with 'Business Teams' representing different constituent businesses to assess current business performance and estimating growth prospects, with SWOT Analysis, and reaching a consensus on 'Solutions' and Action.

2.6. A Second FMB Group Meeting where the Advisor will make a presentation on the results of the 'One-on-One' and Individual Business Team Meetings, and make 'Recommendations for Future Action', to bring about the desired change. At this point, once the FMB Group agrees with the Recommendations, with or without changes, the Implementation Phase will begin.

2.7. The FMB Group will now be active in working with the Consultant on Implementation.

3. Please note that all my efforts as your Advisor will be to assist the FMB Group arrive at the most productive solutions based on ideas originating from each one of its members, of each one of the Group's businesses, and from conclusions arrived at each FMB Group Meeting. This is to ensure that all members of the FMB Group are actively involved and committed to make the desired solutions happen.

4. During this process, the Advisor is available to all FMB Group Members, individually, on video calls and on telephone, 24x7, to help with greater understanding of issues and processes, on clarifications required, and to listen to their views on any issue. All these will be active inputs for bringing about solutions that will finally enhance the well-being of the Family, enrich professional capabilities of all who constitute the members of the FMB Group, and of performance of the individual enterprises, and finally of the Family Business as a whole.

TIERRRA©
TRUST
INTEGRITY
ETHICS
RELATIONSHIPS
REPUTATION
RESULTS
ACCOUNTABILITY
CORE VALUES FOR A FAMILY BUSINESS

Copyright © 2018 Raju Swamy/ PROMAG Consultancy Services/ April 13, 2015
All Rights Reserved

www.ingramcontent.com/pod-product-compliance
Lightning Source LLC
Chambersburg PA
CBHW020904180526

45163CB00007B/2624